Sicilia

Sicilia

Ben Tish

Photography by
Kris Kirkham

BLOOMSBURY ABSOLUTE
LONDON · OXFORD · NEW YORK · NEW DELHI · SYDNEY

introduction

Sicilia is my letter of love to one of the oldest, most richly varied food cultures in Europe.

Sicily is a frustratingly complex contradiction in terms. At once both a frugal, peasant land with a simple, robust cuisine yet also a land full of ornate glamour and shameless extravagance. There isn't a country that I know with a richer or more diverse tapestry of cultural influences.

I've spent much time exploring the regions of the mainland as well as the otherworldly island groupings off Sicily's coast – the Aeolian and the Egadi. And every time I visit, I discover something new and wonderful.

Sicily sits at the true heart of the Mediterranean, between east and west, Europe and North Africa. As such it is perhaps no wonder that the island's cuisine is so richly diverse. The Moorish and Norman occupation of the island brought culinary innovations and advanced cooking techniques in tandem with the introduction of exotic fruits and vegetables to an already abundant and fertile soil – citrus, almonds and spices mixing harmoniously with the simple indigenous olives, vines and wheat.

This book explores the island through its food. I have featured a favourite selection of traditional dishes, both simple and extravagant, as well as other dishes that I've created, inspired by Sicily's bountiful produce, cooking styles and gloriously sun-soaked Mediterranean way of life.

The recipes within are in the main simple, sometimes no more than an assembly of beautiful ingredients, whilst others might be more time consuming but always eminently achievable with careful planning.

the african kiss

Sicily's history is rich, complex and diverse. It has experienced many years under various occupations including the Romans, Normans, Spaniards, French and Visigoth Greeks. Each occupier has left a little bit of their culture. However, for me it is the footprint of the Moors and the Berbers that has left the strongest mark.

It was on my first visit to the wild and sensual Palermo with its souk-like markets, noisy haggling, vibrant colours, evocative Arabic architecture and diverse demographics that first inspired me to write my book *Moorish*. In *Moorish* I focused not just on the better-known Moorish Andalusian cuisine of southern Spain but also on the wonderful cooking of Moorish-influenced Sicily.

Sicily, often thought of as the crossroads of Europe and as a strategically important gateway, found itself under Arab rule at the start of the 9th century. The Arab rule passed through various dynastic families until in

948 Hasan al-Kalbi declared himself Emir of Sicily, though quite soon rival 'emirates' were established in Enna and Syracuse. The island was then divided into three administrative districts, whose names survive still – di Mazara, Val di Noto and Val di Demone.

The Arab world was arguably the most advanced civilisation of its time and Sicily certainly benefited from becoming part of it, not least in terms of agriculture and culinary matters. It soon entered a period of great cultural enlightenment and economic progress, the benefits of which are seen and felt to this day.

In agriculture, the new rulers moved to diversify production and introduce new crops, including dates, lemons and sugar cane, all harnessed by a radical and very effective irrigation system.

The Arab influence is still seen today, particularly within Sicilian cuisine – almonds, saffron, oranges, pistachio and pomegranates amongst many others, bear witness to their influence.

Many sweets retain clear Arab influence, using nuts as replacements for flour and honey to replace sugar, and adding fragrant flower waters for flavour. The highly skilled, forward-looking Arab cooks were adept at creating complex and highly designed confections. They created layers of vibrant colours, added preserving fruits to syrups to enhance the visual impact of cakes, biscuits and sweets. And all was carried out on the instruction of the Arab rulers and the monied classes. The extravagance that was on display then is still evident in Sicilian confections today. Sorbets and *granite* also owe their popularity to North African ingenuity, cleverly designed to combat the summer heat.

One of the most common dishes in western Sicily is couscous (or cus cus). It is celebrated each year at the end of September when San Vito Lo Capo hosts an international couscous festival. The west coast fishing town of Trapani has a seafood version close to my heart – the seafood is deliciously poached in a rich stock scented with saffron and cinnamon and the couscous is stirred in just before eating, making for a hearty, nourishing lunch for the hard-working local fishermen.

The Arabs also promoted saffron more widely, helping it to become an elegant spice of choice in the Middle Ages, where it was commonly used to colour and subtly flavour classic Sicilian dishes like arancini and *pasta*

con le sarde (pasta with sardines, pine nuts raisins and fennel).

And using their manufacturing skills, the Sicilian Arabs moved into mass production of dried pasta.

Amazingly, despite the banning of alcohol under Muslim law, the Zibibbo grape, used to make Passito di Pantelleria, the supreme dessert wine, was introduced to the island by the Arabs. They also encouraged the distillation of alcohol to produce sweet smelling perfumes eventually moving on to the production of grappa-style eaux de vie.

Even cooking techniques, now common place, such as controlled cooking over fire and deep-frying in oil, were introduced by the Arab chefs with the locals taking to these new and ground-breaking skills as if to their own – these are techniques that are still widely used today.

When asked what it was that first made me fall for Sicily and its glorious cuisine, I say it was the beautiful nature of the Arab-Italian fusion and the way it perfectly reflects the muddled nature of modern life.

the food markets

I never tire of exploring the food markets of Sicily. They assault the senses with noise, colour, hustle, bustle, smoke and produce so strikingly vibrant and almost surreal that it knocks me back.

I remember the first time my wife Nykeeta and I visited Palermo and wandered into the Ballaro street market. It felt like being in a North African souk. Exotic piles of spices, soot-faced stall holders grilling vegetables and meat over billowing charcoal, vendors shouting and gesticulating and a mix of eager, wide-eyed tourists rubbing shoulders with locals, both young and old, haggling, bantering, laughing and eating.

Everything in the Ballaro seems bigger and bolder than anywhere else. Squashes several feet long, huge alien-like glistening tomatoes slowly cooking in the sun, vast tubs of prepared spikey artichokes ready to be taken home and cooked instantly, tangles of vibrant, ultra-green turnip tops. The many varieties of citrus – blood oranges, meyer lemons, green satsumas, gigantic Cedro lemons to be eaten, skin, pith and all, highly-scented bergamots and bags of lemon and orange leaves for infusing in stews or for scenting meatballs. And to reinforce the feeling of being in a North African souk, exotic stalls of purple and white aubergines, pomegranates, ripe black figs, dates and fresh almonds.

Swordfish and tuna glistening in the sun, the fishmonger slicing pieces off the gigantic bodies. Octopus and varieties of fresh prawns sold by the handful and stuffed into used carrier bags to take home. Rough and ready but all the more charming for it.

At the butchers' counters, offal and the extremities are the most popular cuts on display. Lungs, spleen, brains, tails, trotters and snouts take centre stage, harking back to a time when only the elite of Sicilian society could afford the prime cuts. And don't be surprised if you see horse meat for sale – it's still one of the most popular meats on the island.

The market is full of stalls selling delicious and sometimes challenging freshly cooked fast food to eat as you go. If you visit the market early, avoiding the sweltering summer heat, you'll find fry shops selling *panelle*, the chickpea flour fritters fried in olive oil, and perhaps potato croquettes flecked with fresh mint and orange zest. And for a hearty treat to set you up for the day, Sfinconi, the Sicilian pizza, layered with tomato, ricotta, pecorino and fresh herbs. The tripe vendors will also be doing a booming trade – seeded buns with warm braised tripe from hot hold boxes finished with squeezes of fresh lemon or *pane ca meusa*, similar to the tripe buns but made with boiled spleen, fried in pork fat and stuffed into a sesame seed roll.

But for me it is the *stiggihole* that give the market it's singular atmosphere. Skewers of sheep's guts grilled over wood and charcoal until blackened and then finished with fresh parsley, lemon and salt. The smoke from the grills mixing with the sweet farmyard-like aroma hanging heavy in the air, the skilful grillers taking pride in wafting the smoke through the market to let you know that you are in Sicily – and only Sicily.

And then there are the sweet treats. Incredible piles and buckets of candied and dried fruits, bejewelled biscuits made with nuts and spices and *mostarda di mosti* – the Sicilian chewy sweets made from reduced grape must mixed with nuts and spices. Fried pastry stall holders will be seen crouching

over vast saucepans of bubbling oil, frying the pieces of dough until golden brown, sifting them out and quickly dousing them in sugar, honey or orange flower water. Delicious to munch whilst thinking about lunch.

Tourism has diluted the market experience to some degree but the big four markets of Palermo – Bullaro, Capo, Borgo Vecchio and Vucciria – and Catania's Fera o luni, held in a grand baroque square, are still the real deal. And much fun and brilliant chaos can be discovered in the street markets of Syracuse on the east coast and Marsala on the west coast, where the Arabic influence is most strongly felt with Tunisia just a short hop across the water.

The street food markets of Sicily are a way of life and the beating heart of the island, and I love them.

a quick trip: sicily's islands

As well as being the largest island in the Mediterranean, Sicily also encompasses the many smaller satellite islands in the Ionian, Mediterranean and Tyrrhenian Seas. These dazzling islands, comprising three archipelagos and several standalone formations, remain unknown to most travellers. Some of these stunningly beautiful and otherworldly islands are barely inhabited, nothing more than a fishing village or two. I've been lucky to spend some time travelling and eating around the islands – both the well-known Aeolians in the north-west and the less familiar Pantellaria and Pelagie off the south-west coast.

My wife and I first visited the islands together about seven years ago. We took a boat from mainland Sicily to Salina. On arrival we were struck by the contrast. Sicily's hustling bustling charm had been left behind and we were greeted by peace and serenity. Pastel-coloured stucco houses dot the island landscape and a few bars and restaurants appear here and there. Stunning beaches and a sun-baked volcanic terrain enchant the eye. Even at the height of the season, tourists are few and far between.

And then there's the very special food – wonderful dishes and produce specific to the Aeolian islands. The waters are rich with seafood and the land fertile, able to grow gigantic and flavoursome vegetables and vines that produce some of the best wines to be found in the Mediterranean, such as Malvasia and Nero d'Avola.

Locally caught fish is the staple. Plump silvery sardines can be found cooking on the bone over dried rosemary twigs to charred perfection all along the beaches and outside restaurants. The smoky rosemary aroma wafts across the islands evoking the sultry magic of the place. A specific type of brown squid called *totani* is one of the main hauls for local fishermen, very meaty with a strong flavour, quite unique and to be grilled over charcoal and sprinkled with local lemon juice, salt and dried oregano leaves. Super fresh salty scorpion fish is eaten *crudo*-style with just a squeeze of orange or lemon juice and a sprinkling of salt. On one memorable visit to Salina at the wonderful house-cum-restaurant of chef Carla Rando we were cooked a whole spatola, a fish similar to bream, in a fried bread crust with orange zest – it was delicious and summed up the island's easy approach to cooking the best ingredients without fuss and with simplicity.

Mulberry trees are abundant. The juicy, heavy-perfumed fruits are found thrown into salads or turned into refreshing *granita* and ice cream. Courgette flowers are everywhere in the summer months – fried and steamed – along with purple aubergines and tomatoes beyond compare.

Hardly anything on the islands is imported, even from the mainland. Many homes will make their own ricotta or ricotta salata (the hard, dried variety used for grating). Vegetables are grown and sometimes supplied to nearby restaurants.

My first experience of the fabled Aeolian tomato came beach side at the famous Da Alfredo restaurant in Salina in the form of a *pane cuzanto*. Warm garlicky bread piled high with tomatoes, green olives, anchovies and the island's famous salty capers, all washed down with a bottle of Salina's dry Malvasia that harnessed all the flavours and aromas of the Mediterranean. A selection of local citrus *granite* followed to refresh us in the baking July sun. It was simple, almost basic, but with flavours of such intensity and vibrancy that it knocked me back and the memory has stayed me with ever since.

On the same trip we headed over to the island of Pantelleria, known as the black pearl of the Mediterranean, just a few miles off the Tunisian coast. An island undiscovered by tourists with a more rugged feel to it than those of the Aeolians. Again, fish is the order of the day, with braises and stews of mixed fish and shellfish spiked with aromatics and spices, served with couscous. Saffron features heavily in the spicing of rice and pasta sauces. In a small restaurant we were served a glorious spaghetti pasta with a sauce made from fish stock, ground almonds, saffron and clams – perfection!

Pantelleria has its own pesto made from chopped fresh tomatoes, herbs, almonds and olives which is then tossed through pasta and finished with breadcrumbs. The island is also well known for its sweet passito wines made from Zibbibo grapes that are left to dehydrate in the sun to intensify the flavour and sweetness – utterly delicious when accompanying the island's signature dish *baci panteschi*, or kissing biscuits (see page 228). After a couple of days island hopping, we reached our final stop of Lampedusa in the Pelagie. It is best known for its incredible beaches and in particular the stunning

Rabbit Beach. Parts of this small island are akin to a more tropical location with many palms, cactus, yuccas, figs and olives growing in the fertile soil.

Fish on Lampedusa is almost only cooked two ways: either baked whole or in fillets in a salt crust, the salt taken from local flats, or in an intense tomato sauce with the addition of potatoes, olives and capers. Caciocavallo cheese is very popular here and the locals like to fry it in olive oil and drizzle it with honey and a sprinkle of pistachio nuts. It's quite delicious. Meat is almost non-existent and in dishes where you might expect meat you are likely to find aubergines or squashes, usually swathed in sweet and sour sauces. Before leaving the island, we ate a memorable blancmange-like dessert which was basically sweet milk set with cornflour and flavoured with spices such as cinnamon, cloves and ginger. You are given the option of three toppings, either chocolate, pistachios or more cinnamon – I went for all three.

The islands of Sicily are enchanting. Take the time to visit them and you will be rewarded with a close-up view of Sicily's extraordinary culinary heritage set amidst the most beautiful scenery and amongst the most interesting and friendly people.

the holy grail

Being a chef isn't just about cooking food for hungry customers at a restaurant. Being a chef is an all-consuming lifestyle that dictates the direction of your days off. Luckily my amazing wife Nykeeta seems to put up with it – not least because she's a foodie but also because she has the patience of a saint and is able to accept without complaint my borderline obsessive food-focused exploits.

Together we have travelled to many far flung and often difficult to reach locations around the world on the promise of the best meal ever known to man or woman. This expectation can bring many disappointments. However, sometimes it's well worth the time and effort involved. Before one of our last excursions to Sicily, I had been told of a restaurant that was reportedly serving the best pasta in Sicily with wonderful Etna wines at a fraction of the price you might find elsewhere. This was to be our Holy Grail.

Terra Mia is located on the northern slopes of Mount Etna in Solicchiata. Research into the restaurant was near impossible with very little information online and a website that included just one dish from the menu – a pasta with truffle. All I had to go on were recommendations. But I warmed to the idea and had a good feeling about this adventure.

Once found we instantly fell in love with Terra Mia. It's a beautiful old farmhouse set back in shaded woodlands, surrounded by vineyards. The restaurant is set within the farmhouse, home to Mara Fiorista and chef Leonardo Cuscona, a lovely, passionate couple who greeted us on arrival for our spring lunch. It was off season and quiet with just five or six other tables. The owners either make everything themselves or source produce within walking distance of the farmhouse. The sea is 18 miles away so no seafood here!

We began our meal with a glass of bone dry, minerally, Etna bianco, typical of the grapes found growing in the unique volcanic-mineral rich soil. The menu was short. Homemade focaccia and sheep's milk ricotta with local blossom honey and pistachios and then a plate of the most delicious fennel salami from the owners own Nebrodi pigs, made with fennel pollen rather than the more usual rough seeds. It was an exercise in simplicity and flavour.

And so, to the pasta.

One fresh egg pasta ravioli, unusual for Sicily where dried water pasta is predominant due to the climate. On asking why, they said that as it was a cool spring it was easy to make. The ravioli were filled with local sautéed greens, caciocavallo cheese and dried chilli, simply finished with a first press extra virgin olive. There was also a spaghetti with the freshest almonds, wild fennel fronds and dried-salted grapes left from a harvest. This was perhaps the best pasta I've ever had. You could say the holy grail of pasta, summing up Sicily's culinary ethos in a simple bowl of deliciousness.

We drank a bottle of wonderful Tenuta delle Terre Nere 2016, made from 100-year-old vines growing just around the corner from the farmhouse, costing only a few euros. It was a new wine to me but one that I sourced immediately on my return to London for sale in my restaurant and personal consumption at home.

A no choice dessert produced a bowl of mulberries that looked like they might burst in front of us, such was their ripeness, and a bowl of milk with a yellow crust, so rich and thick it was almost like double cream. The milk was to be poured over the mulberries and then crushed lightly to make a sort of mulberry milkshake. The mulberries had been picked the day before having been slowly baked in the Sicilian spring sun and oozed their sweet, aromatic Mediterranean flavours through the milk-rich dessert.

That whole wonderful, memorable, afternoon spent on Mount Etna was indeed the holy grail. Now we are in search of the next one...

bread

Sicily has long held a stellar reputation for the quality of its bread and its bakers – the breadbasket of Europe some have claimed.

Despite famine and plague over past centuries the island now proudly celebrates its love affair with wheat through a resurgence in the growth of wonderful artisan bakers celebrating and rediscovering the ancient varieties of wheat.

At the last count there were estimated to be over 50 varieties of wheat being grown across Sicily, with artisan bakers reclaiming long-forgotten flavours sacrificed to the requirements of industrialised breadmaking needed to satisfy the demands of supermarket shelves.

These different wheats, which are grown inland all over the island, are baked into breads in wood-fired ovens using a variety of woods, producing a cornucopia of flavours. They are now being gently rolled out to eager Sicilians delighting in new flavours and textures.

Some of the more widely used wheats to be found are Biancolilla, Bidi, Perciasacchi, Rusello and Tumminia, to name just a few. These varieties, and all the many others, have their own distinctive flavour and aromas. Although they are sometimes difficult to work with, they produce wonderful and life-affirming results for the Sicilian table.

Pane cuzanto is probably Sicily's most popular bread preparation – consisting of freshly baked Sicilian bread topped with fresh tomatoes, olive oil, basil, oregano and black pepper. It is incredibly simple but when made with a freshly baked, chewy loaf and exceptional tomatoes and oil it is a thing of beauty.

It is said the best *pane cuzanto* to be found on the island is in Scopello, a tiny coastal village near Trapani. The bakery doesn't have a name, but it is the only one there. I've yet to try it but it's on my list for the next visit!

The Mafalda recipe on page 20 is as authentic as I could get without actually baking in a wood oven, over almond shells in Sicily. The sesame seeds are ubiquitous on Sicilian breads – a throwback from the island's Arabic occupation. It's the real deal and as crunchy and chewy as you could wish for.

Another traditional use, which I delight in as it's so typical of Sicily, is the dipping of the bread into red wine and sugar to be given to children as a treat. I love it, it is delicious and far too good for children!

The famed pane squarato bread of Marsala, which is boiled before it's baked, similar to a bagel, is flavoured with spices and often served at the major religious festivals, adorned with four rosettes. When and if found it should be bought and relished with delight.

The breads within this chapter are a mix of tradition and inspiration – all requiring some time and patience but all easily achievable. I really can't think of a better way to spend a Saturday than preparing, proving and baking bread – the aromas and anticipation are as exciting as the eating. Enjoy!

Mafalda

Mafalda bread is probably the most well-known and popular bread used throughout the whole region. It's typified by its rich golden crust, the rich nutty flavour from the semolina and the sesame seeds with which it's finished. Mafalda is said to have Arabic origins and that a baker from Catania created it for an Italian queen, Mafalda di Savoia.

The bread is often formed into the shape of a serpent but has different guises and can be found in the shape of a crown or even with slits to represent the eyes of Saint Lucia. Delicious stuffed with the chickpea *panelle* on page 54.

Makes 1 large loaf, about 800g

For the starter
100g strong white flour
100ml lukewarm water
30g sourdough starter

For the dough
15g fresh yeast
300ml lukewarm water

250g wholemeal flour
250g semolina flour
1 tablespoon extra virgin olive oil
  plus extra for brushing
2 teaspoons fine sea salt
1 egg yolk for brushing
1 teaspoon sesame seeds

The day before you will make the dough, prepare the starter: mix the strong flour with the water and sourdough starter, stirring well. Leave the bowl at room temperature, uncovered, to slowly ferment and bubble for 12 hours.

The next day, mix the fresh yeast with the lukewarm water and set it aside to activate for a few minutes or until frothy. Put the flours, olive oil and salt into a stand mixer and mix in the fermented starter and the yeast mixture. Knead in the machine for a couple of minutes to bring together into a very soft dough. Transfer the dough to a bowl and set aside for 30 minutes. (Alternatively, you can mix and knead the dough by hand.)

Now turn the dough on to a floured surface. Fold the dough over a couple of times, then place back in the bowl. Put into a plastic bag or cover with clingfilm. Leave to rise in a room not warmer than 18°C for 12 hours – do not put the dough into the fridge.

After 12 hours, shape the bread into a serpent or a crown by gently folding it as opposed to kneading it, which would take out the air. Place on a baking tray and leave to rest for 30 minutes.

Preheat the oven to 240°C/220°C fan/Gas Mark 9. Brush the bread with egg yolk and sprinkle with the sesame seeds. Cut lines into the dough at 5cm intervals.

Put the bread into the oven and add some steam with a spray of water. Quickly close the oven door. After 10 minutes, open the oven door and let the steam out. Now cut into the lines in the dough again. Turn the temperature down to 220°C/200°C fan/Gas Mark 7 and bake for a further 30 minutes. The bread should sound hollow when the base is tapped. Brush with olive oil and bake for a final 2–3 minutes – the bread will be golden brown with a crunchy crust. Transfer to a wire rack to cool.

Focaccia

Focaccia is steeped in ancient history. It is first official documented in Ancient Rome as a simple flat bread, cooked hearth side and smothered in olive oil, spices and herbs. Now, whilst eaten all over Italy it's mainly associated with Liguria, where it has many variants from town to town.

I've eaten my fair share of this most delicious of breads, travelling around Italy and developing my recipe for Norma. It's the only bread that we serve at Norma and we make it twice a day, every day. The recipe is packed with Sicilian influences – fragrant herbs, pine nuts and green olives. The inclusion of olive oil is unusual but adds a wonderful depth of flavour to the bread and an intrinsic seasoning. I use a delicious, fresh Nocellara extra virgin olive oil from Sicily, but you could use any good-quality extra virgin.

Serves 10–12

375g strong white flour
375g '00' pasta flour
1 tablespoon fine sea salt
a 7g sachet dried yeast
100ml extra virgin olive oil
  plus extra for brushing
about 400ml lukewarm water
a good handful of pine nuts
2 tablespoons coarse semolina

For the topping
2 tablespoons extra virgin olive oil
2 tablespoons water
150g pitted green olives, halved, plus
  2 tablespoons of the olive brine
1 teaspoon Maldon sea salt flakes
a handful of marjoram or
  oregano leaves
a handful of mint leaves

Put the flours into a large mixing bowl with the salt and yeast. Whisk well to combine, then make a hole in the middle and add the olive oil and 300ml water. Stir together, adding more water (I used about 100ml extra) until you have a very soft, but not too sticky, dough. Mix in two-thirds of the pine nuts.

Now knead the dough until soft and elastic, preferably in a stand mixer on a medium-slow speed for about 7 minutes. Alternatively, knead by hand on a lightly oiled work surface for 10–12 minutes. Put the dough on a lightly oiled rimless baking sheet and leave to rise in a draught-free place for 1–1½ hours or until roughly doubled in size.

Knock back the dough. Lightly dust the baking tray with the semolina. Gently press the dough out with your fingers to fit the baking tray. Brush with olive oil and leave to rise again for about 1 hour or until doubled in size again. When this time has nearly elapsed, preheat the oven to 240°C/220°C fan/Gas Mark 9 and put a pizza stone or baking tray in there to heat up. If you have a water spray, ready it.

For the topping, whisk together the olive oil, water and olive brine until emulsified. Transfer the dough to the hot pizza stone or baking tray and poke dimples into the surface of the dough with your fingertips. Pour the oil-brine mixture over the top and scatter on the salt flakes. Press in the marjoram or oregano, mint and olives. Slide the pizza stone or tray back into the oven. Squirt a little water into the bottom of the oven, then quickly close the oven door and bake for 25–30 minutes or until the focaccia is golden on top and sounds hollow when tapped on the base. Transfer the focaccia to a wire rack and leave to cool slightly for 10 minutes. Serve while still warm.

Fig and Fennel Bread

An aromatic, sweet-savoury bread that's quick and easy to make. I like to serve this lightly grilled, spread with ricotta and drizzled with honey for a delicious breakfast.

Makes 2 loaves

1 tablespoon golden caster sugar
a 7g sachet dried yeast
300ml lukewarm water
200g dried figs, quartered
150g fresh ripe figs, roughly chopped
50g dried cherries
375g strong white flour
60g rye flour

60g wholemeal flour
1½ tablespoons fennel seeds
1 tablespoon pumpkin seeds
2 teaspoons fine sea salt
olive oil for drizzling
coarse polenta for dusting
butter and plain flour for the tins

In a small bowl mix together the sugar and yeast with the warm water. Allow the mixture to prove for 10 minutes or until golden bubbles rise to the surface.

Combine all the remaining ingredients, apart from the olive oil and polenta, in a large mixing bowl and toss together, coating the figs and cherries well with the flours. Add the yeast mixture all at once and stir vigorously with a wooden spoon. Transfer the dough to a flour-dusted work surface and knead for 5 minutes.

Transfer the dough to a clean mixing bowl. Drizzle with olive oil and turn over to coat. Cover the bowl with clingfilm and leave to rise at room temperature for an hour or until the dough has doubled in size. (You can also leave it to rise overnight in the fridge.)

Turn the dough out on to a work surface and knead gently for 1–2 minutes. Leave to rest for a minute while you butter and flour two 450g loaf tins. Set aside.

Cut the dough in half. Shape each half into a ball and roll in the polenta, then place in the tins. Cover with a tea towel and leave to rise for 40 minutes.

Preheat the oven to 200°C/180°C fan/Gas Mark 6.

Sprinkle the top of each loaf with water, then place the tins in the oven. Immediately reduce the oven temperature to 190°C/170°C fan/Gas Mark 5. Bake for 40–45 minutes or until the polenta crust is golden and the loaves sound hollow when tapped on the base. Cool on a wire rack for 10 minutes before removing from the tins.

Sicilian Brioche

I'd heard about these sweet Brioche breakfast sandwiches filled with *gelato* or *granita* before I had ever set foot in Sicily – in my mind they were already legendary and deeply desirable.

I mean, really – a soft, citrus-scented brioche bun stuffed with a strong espresso *granita* and whipped cream and eaten before going to work! How could you not be impressed by this outrageous breakfast? At Norma, my Sicilian-inspired restaurant in London, we make these daily, in the traditional way with the little *tuppe* on top and we stuff them with pistachio ice cream and finish with chocolate sauce. The brioche moulds make things easier for the bake and keep the shape consistent.

They don't, however, get served for breakfast – they are on the menu as a dessert and are extremely popular!

Makes 8

2 large free-range eggs
100g unsalted butter, at room temperature, plus extra for greasing
2 teaspoons fine sea salt
400g strong white flour
100g '00' pasta flour
100g caster sugar

zest of 1 orange
a 7g sachet dried yeast
200ml full-fat milk

To glaze
1 free-range egg, beaten
granulated sugar

Put the eggs, butter, salt, flours, sugar, orange zest and yeast into the bowl of a stand mixer. Combine using the whisk attachment, then gradually add the milk to form a very sticky dough. The process should take around 15 minutes. (Alternatively, you can mix the dough by hand.)

Cover the bowl with a cloth and leave to rise in a warm place for 3–4 hours or until doubled in size (this dough has a slow rise but is all the better for it).

Preheat the oven to 200°C/180°C fan/Gas Mark 6. Lightly grease eight 75mm mini brioche moulds.

Divide the dough into 8 portions. Remove a small piece from each portion (about 10g) and roll all of the pieces into balls. Make an indentation in the top of each large ball and place a smaller ball in this – like a cherry on the top.

Place the shaped brioches in the moulds. Brush with the beaten egg to glaze and sprinkle with granulated sugar. Bake for 25 minutes or until golden. Remove from the oven and leave to rest in the moulds until cool enough to handle, then transfer to a wire rack to cool completely.

Bignolati
Sicilian sausage bread ring with fennel seeds

The *bignolati* hails from the Agrigento region on the island's south side. It is traditionally a Sunday centrepiece for a family gathering and usually made by the nonna. The original recipes uses unleavened dough but I've lightened it, proved the dough and spiked the pork mince filling with capers and fennel seeds. It's delicious served with salsa verde or alioli to dip (see page 280 and 283).

Serves about 12

For the dough
20g fresh yeast
500ml lukewarm water
50ml extra virgin olive oil plus extra
25g fine sea salt
a pinch of sugar
500g plain flour
500g semolina flour

For the filling
olive oil for cooking
2 onions, finely sliced

1 garlic clove, finely chopped
400g pork sausage meat (or meat
    from quality pork sausages)
1 tablespoon fennel seeds
1 tablespoon miniature capers
a large handful of fennel herb,
    wild fennel fronds or dill
70g raisins, soaked in warm water
    to plump up
sea salt and freshly ground
    black pepper

Combine the yeast and warm water in a large bowl (or the bowl of a stand mixer). Set aside to prove for about 10 minutes.

Add the olive oil, salt, sugar and flours. Mix by hand until a dough is formed, then knead for about 10 minutes or until the dough is smooth and elastic.

Alternatively, if using a stand mixer, use the dough hook on low speed to mix the oil, salt, sugar and flours into the yeast liquid for 1 minute. Increase to medium speed and knead for 7 minutes.

Transfer the dough to a large bowl lightly coated with olive oil and turn it once to coat both sides with oil. Cover with clingfilm and leave to rise in a warm place until doubled in size, about 1 hour.

For the filling, heat a lug of olive oil in a large sauté pan over a medium heat and gently cook the onions and garlic until softened and lightly browned. Add the sausage meat and fennel seeds and cook for 7–8 minutes or until cooked through. Finish with the capers, fennel herb and drained raisins. Season. Stir well to combine, then leave to cool.

Once the dough has risen, transfer it to a well-floured work surface. Begin flattening the dough using the tips of your fingers to stretch it out. Next, use a rolling pin to roll out the dough into a rectangle about 24 x 16cm. If necessary, turn the dough so it is lying horizontally on the work surface in front of you.

...continued on page 30

Evenly spread the filling over the dough, leaving a 2.5cm edge clear all around the outside. Roll up the dough like a swiss roll, beginning at the long edge nearest to you. Once rolled, cut off excess loose dough from each end.

Transfer the rolled dough to a baking tray lined with baking parchment. Curve both ends round to connect and form a ring. Cut slits in the top (to release steam during cooking). Cover and leave to rest for 1 hour.

Preheat the oven to 210°C/190°C fan/Gas Mark 6/7.

Bake for 20 minutes, then reduce the oven to 200°C/180°C fan/Gas Mark 6 and bake for a further 20–25 minutes or until golden. Cool for about 15 minutes before cutting into slices.

Scaccia
Sicilian lasagna bread

This wonderful street food bread is hugely popular in its native Ragusa and is a baking masterclass combining rustic simplicity with incredibly delicious indulgence. The mountainside community of Ragusa, with white stone cube buildings which would not be out of place in North Africa, is home to a famous bakery called Giummarra, renowned for producing the best *scaccia* in all the land. I chatted to the baker there on a visit and he told me that apparently the *scaccia* is a distant relation to the Tunisian Brik – albeit baked rather than deep fried.

My homemade version is a result of many trials and errors, but I'm happy to say that I think it's on a par with Giummarra!

Serves 4–6

For the dough
250g strong white flour
250g semolina flour
6g fine sea salt
10g fresh yeast
1 teaspoon caster sugar
300–330ml lukewarm water
2 tablespoons olive oil plus extra
    for brushing

For the filling
1 tablespoon olive oil
2 onions, finely diced
1 garlic clove, finely chopped
500g cherry tomatoes, cut into quarters
a large handful of basil, leaves picked
    and torn
150g provolone or caciocavallo cheese,
    finely sliced
sea salt and freshly ground black pepper

Put the flours into a bowl with the salt and mix well. Mix the yeast and sugar with 100ml of the water, stirring until dissolved. Make a well in the flour and slowly add a little of the remaining water, incorporating the flour from the sides. Add the yeast mixture, oil and a little more water to the well and mix in more flour from the sides. Continue until all the flour has been incorporated and you have a soft rough dough.

Rub a little olive oil on your work surface. Tip the dough on to it and knead for 10 minutes or so or until the dough is smooth and silky. Place in a clean bowl, cover and leave to rise for at least 1 hour or until the dough has doubled in size. The longer the rise the better, as the flavour will improve over time.

While the dough is rising, prepare the filling. Heat the olive oil in a medium pan over a medium heat and sauté the onions and garlic gently until soft but without colour. Add the cherry tomatoes, season well and stir. Cook for a further 10 minutes or until the tomatoes begin to break down into a chunky sauce. Remove from the heat and leave to cool. Once cool stir through the picked basil.

...continued on page 32

Preheat the oven to 220°C/200°C fan/Gas Mark 7. Line a baking tray with baking parchment.

When the dough is ready, tip it on to a floured work surface. Roll out into a large circle about 80cm diameter and 4mm thick. Spread three-quarters of the tomato filling over the dough, leaving a clear border of about 4cm around the edge. Cover with three-quarters of the cheese. Fold in 2 opposite sides of the dough circle so the edges meet in the middle.

Spread the remaining tomato filling down the centre to cover the join followed by the remaining cheese. Now fold in the opposite ends so they cover 2cm of dough. Starting with the end furthest away from you fold the dough over to make a neat parcel (see picture).

Place on a baking tray and brush with olive oil. Bake for 35–40 minutes or until crisp and golden. Leave to cool before slicing.

I suggest serving the scaccia street-food style, wrapped in greaseproof paper and washed down with a cold beer.

Impanata Catanese
Sicilian cheese and cauliflower bread 'pie'

This is similar to the lasagna bread, Scaccia (see page 31), but uses a stronger dough and, typical to Catania, roasted cauliflowers with pine nuts and raisins. It's similar to a Spanish *empanada* and was most likely developed when Sicily was under Spanish rule.

The *impanata Catanese* is traditionally eaten at dinner on Christmas Eve but Catania's street vendors have this version all year round, feeding the hungry locals and tourists alike.

Serves 4

a 7g sachet dried yeast
400ml lukewarm water
1 teaspoon honey
700g semolina flour
4 tablespoons extra virgin olive oil
   plus extra for drizzling
1 teaspoon fine sea salt
1 cauliflower, cored, florets and leaves
   finely sliced

60g pitted green olives
30g toasted pine nuts
30g raisins, soaked in warm water
   to plump and drained
400g provolone cheese, cut into cubes
50g Parmesan cheese, finely grated
sea salt and freshly ground
   black pepper

Dissolve the yeast in 300ml of the warm water along with the honey. Sift the flour into a large bowl, make a well in the centre and add the extra virgin olive oil, salt and yeast mixture. Stir with a wooden spoon to form a rough dough, adding the rest of the water as you go.

Transfer the dough to a work surface and knead until smooth and elastic. Place in a bowl, cover with clingfilm and leave to rise for about 1 hour or until the dough doubles in size.

Preheat the oven to 220°C/200°C fan/Gas Mark 7. Oil a 26 x 35cm baking tin and set aside.

Place the cauliflower and leaves in a roasting tin, drizzle with extra virgin olive oil and season. Roast for 30 minutes or until tender and caramelised. Cool (leave the oven on).

Divide the dough in half and roll out one piece into a thin rectangle. Transfer the dough rectangle to the prepared baking tin and use wet hands to mould the dough to fit the tin.

Spread the cauliflower, olives, pine nuts and raisins over the dough and season with extra virgin olive oil, salt and pepper. Finish with the provolone and Parmesan.

Roll out the second piece of dough in the same way and place on top of the cauliflower and cheese filling. Seal all the edges, then brush the top with extra virgin olive oil. Bake for 30 minutes.

Once cooked, allow the impanata to cool for 15 minutes before cutting into squares for serving.

Sfincione

Sicilian-style pizza

The *sfincione*, which has its origins in focaccia, is a deep-dish style 'pizza' baked a in a rectangular or square tray rather than rounds, and is at its most simple and authentic when just topped with tomatoes and fried onion sauce, Ragusano cheese and extra virgin olive oil. It's ubiquitous in Sicily and is a popular choice for Sicily's food market visitors, being sold by vendors in surrounding streets. Everyone has their own little tweak to the classic recipe, which of course makes theirs the very best in town! My addition of fennel, capers and anchovies is quite delicious.

Serves 8

For the dough
20g fresh yeast
500ml lukewarm water
500g '00' pasta flour
500g semolina flour
25g fine sea salt
50ml extra virgin olive oil

For the topping
30g salted anchovies
250g provolone or caciocavallo
   cheese, grated

100g aged pecorino Ragusano
   cheese, grated
1.5 litres tomato sauce (see page 286)
   or passata
a handful of oregano or marjoram,
   leaves picked
50g capers
½ fennel bulb, very finely sliced on
   a mandoline or with a sharp knife
50ml extra virgin olive oil
sea salt and freshly ground
   black pepper

To make the dough, dissolve the yeast in the water in a large bowl and leave for 5 minutes to activate. Once the yeast has started to foam a little, add the flours and then the salt and oil to make a dough. Knead well until soft and smooth, about 10 minutes. Cover with a damp cloth and leave to rise in a warm spot in the kitchen for 1 hour.

Preheat the oven to 200°C/180°C fan/Gas Mark 6.

Roll out the dough and place in a 30 x 40cm baking tray. Spread the filling ingredients over the dough, first the anchovies, then the cheeses, then the tomato sauce and, finally, the oregano, capers, fennel and extra virgin olive oil. Season. Place in the oven and bake for 25–30 minutes or until the base is cooked through and the topping has started to turn golden brown.

Remove from the oven and cool for 10 minutes before slicing and serving.

Sicilian-style Flattened Bread
with grapes

This recipe is similar to the Tuscan *focaccia schiacciata*, meaning flattened bread. It's quite wine and grape heavy and is popular in the wine growing areas of Sicily where, after the harvest, there are often gluts of overripe or damaged grapes. It can be eaten as a dessert, but I enjoy it with salty cheese such as a pecorino or a blue cheese. And for me, a glass of Nero d'Avola would complete the picture perfectly.

Serves 12

a 7g sachet dried yeast
4 tablespoons Chianti or other dry
red wine
1 tablespoon runny honey
about 175ml lukewarm water
400g '00' pasta flour, or 200g plain
flour and 200g strong flour

60ml extra virgin olive oil (preferably
Sicilian)
½ teaspoon fine sea salt
500g black seedless grapes (I use Sable)
100g caster sugar
icing sugar to finish (optional)

Stir together the yeast, wine, honey and warm water in a large bowl until the yeast has dissolved. Set aside until bubbly, about 10 minutes.

Stir in 150g of the flour (the mixture will be lumpy). Cover the bowl with clingfilm and a kitchen towel and leave to rise in a warm place for 40–50 minutes or until doubled in size.

Add the oil, 200g of the remaining flour and the salt and stir until a sticky dough forms. Knead the dough on a well-floured work surface for 8–10 minutes, gradually adding the remaining flour if necessary to prevent the dough from sticking, until the dough is smooth and elastic but still soft. Transfer the dough to an oiled large bowl and turn to coat. Cover the bowl with clingfilm and leave to rise in a warm place for about 1 hour or until doubled in size.

Turn out the dough on to the work surface and knead several times to release air. Cut the dough in half. Using a lightly floured rolling pin, roll out one piece (keeping the remaining piece covered) into a rough 30 x 25cm rectangle. Lift the dough rectangle into a lightly oiled 38 x 25cm baking tin that is 2.5cm deep. Gently stretch the dough to cover as much of the bottom of the tin as possible (the dough may not fit exactly).

Scatter half of the grapes over the dough, then sprinkle the grapes with half of the caster sugar. Roll out the remaining dough in the same manner and place it on top of the sugared grapes, gently stretching the dough to cover them. Scatter the remaining grapes and caster sugar on top and gently press into the dough. Cover the tin with clingfilm and a kitchen towel and leave to rise in a warm place for 1 hour or until doubled in size.

Preheat the oven to 200°C/180°C fan/Gas Mark 6. Bake the bread in the middle of the oven for 25–30 minutes or until well browned and firm in the middle. Loosen the sides and base of the bread with a spatula and slide on to a wire rack to cool. Serve at room temperature, sprinkled with icing sugar if you like.

Sicilian Lemon and Orange Sweet Bread

This fantastic recipe is based on the traditional Italian Easter cake *colomba de Pasqua*. My Sicilian version is packed with citrus flavours, nuts and cinnamon, bringing rays of sunshine to this sweet bread. Pasticceria Cuccia in Catania makes a similar version to this and is my inspiration. If you get a chance to go, please do as it's quite brilliant – although the charming manager was quite evasive when I started asking for recipes! This recipe could have been placed in the desserts chapter, but Italians consider this strictly a bread. Delicious with a strong coffee and a good limoncello.

Serves 8–10

400g strong white flour plus extra
    for dusting
7g fine sea salt
40g caster sugar
10g dried easy-blend yeast
120ml lukewarm full-fat milk
4 medium free-range eggs, at room
    temperature, lightly whisked
100g unsalted butter, at room
    temperature, cut into small pieces,
    plus extra for greasing
zest of 2 unwaxed lemons
zest of 1 orange

juice of ½ lemon
100g flaked almonds
100g diced mixed candied peel
100g dried cranberries

For the topping
2 medium free-range egg whites
25g caster sugar plus extra
    for sprinkling
20g ground almonds
15g ground pistachios
5g ground cinnamon
50g flaked almonds

Put the flour in a stand mixer fitted with a dough hook. Add the salt and sugar to one side of the bowl and the yeast to the other. Add the milk, eggs and butter and mix on a slow speed for 3 minutes, then on a medium speed for 4 minutes, kneading to make a soft, elastic dough. (Alternatively, you can mix and knead the dough by hand.) Transfer the dough to a bowl, cover and leave to rise for 1 hour.

Grease a 23cm springform cake tin. Mix together the lemon and orange zests, lemon juice, almonds, candied peel and cranberries.

Add the fruit and nut mixture to the risen dough and use your hands to incorporate it evenly. Tip the dough on to a lightly floured surface and shape into a ball. Place in the prepared tin and put into a large, roomy plastic bag. Leave to rise for 3 hours or until the dough has reached the top of the tin.

Preheat the oven to 220°C/200°C fan/Gas Mark 7. Bake the sweet bread on the middle shelf of the oven for 20 minutes.

Meanwhile, for the topping, put the egg whites, sugar, ground almonds, pistachios and cinnamon in a bowl and mix to make a paste. Take the bread out of the oven and spread the almond paste on top (some will run to the sides). Sprinkle with the flaked almonds and a little extra sugar. Lower the oven temperature to 200°C/180°C fan/Gas Mark 6 and bake for a further 20 minutes, covering loosely with foil towards the end of cooking if the bread appears to be browning too much. Leave the sweet bread to cool in the tin for 10 minutes, then release the sides and transfer the bread to a wire rack to cool completely.

fritti

I have a natural affinity with deep fried foods, which most certainly comes from my upbringing in the northern seaside resort of Skegness. A deep-frying mecca if ever there was one and my family owned a large fish and chip cafeteria on the local beach front (where I worked on and off in my youth for pocket money and where, on some level, I suppose my love of food came from). Ninety per cent of the menu would have gone in the fryer at some stage; battered fish and the chips of course, but also burgers, sausages, ham fritters and even pineapple!

While I know, of course, that deep-frying is undoubtedly an unhealthy way to eat, there's no denying it makes most things taste absolutely delicious. There's a magic combination of incredibly fast cooking, at some 180°C, that instantly seals, caramelises and crisps the exterior of the food, and a slow cooking of the inside, almost like steaming, that makes the interior soft and tender. A perfectly fried chip is to me the most obvious example.

Deep-frying plays such a huge part in Sicilian cuisine that I had to dedicate a chapter to all its delicious glory.

The practice, the art some would say, of frying was introduced into Sicily by the Moors and their technically advanced Arab chefs, who would cook their pastries, breads, fish and vegetables in an animal-based fat of lamb or beef. Over time the fats changed to vegetable-based fats such as olive and rapeseed. And when the Muslim rule came to an end the Sicilians turned to flavoursome pork fat in which to cook their arancini and *panelle*.

Deep-frying is a quick and delicious way to cook. Throw any food into searing hot oil and it will quickly develop a golden-brown crunchy crust. Sicilian street food culture is centred around deep frying. The *friggatorie* (fry shops) offer a plethora of inexpensive, fried items to eat on the hoof, most famously arancini (the cheese and meat-laden balls or pear-shaped treats), chickpea *panelle*, potato fritters and *sfinci* (fried dough), of many variations. Fried doughs are either stuffed with savoury meat and vegetables or doused in sugar and syrup. Vegetables such as courgettes, peppers, aubergines and artichokes get dipped in a thick(ish) batter, fried to a deep golden brown and finally sprinkled with sea salt. The deep-fried calzones and pizzas of Catania are legendary – these were the blueprint for the pizzas that we now know and love. And if visiting the island, you will find a few specialists who still fry their doughs in huge vats of olive oil mixed with rapeseed oil.

The common theme, as with other Sicilian peasant foods, is one of making a pig's ear into a silk purse. Their fried foods are low cost, often quite stodgy and always filling, frequently make use of leftovers which, when thrown into the fryer and then sprinkled with salt, produce something delicious! Of course, there's a generalisation here; I've had an equal amount of good and bad fried foods in Sicily, but the best vendors and shops take great pride in their recipes and techniques. The best I've had were around the markets of Ballaro and Capo in Palermo – busy places where things don't hang around for long. I like to have *panella* for breakfast from the ever-busy Friggitoria Chiluzzo, usually sandwiched in a sesame seed bun, and then for lunch perhaps a plate of arancini and some fried vegetables at Bar Scatassa, seeking out some of their wonderful vinegary *caponata* to cut through the oily richness of the arancini.

Nearer the coast it's all about the seafood. I think deep-frying works particularly well for the delicate-fleshed fish and shellfish. Sardines or squid are often lightly dusted in a coarse flour and then plunged into hot oil for a few minutes. The result is a crispy golden outside yielding to a steaming hot and tender inside, which is served simply with fresh lemon and lots of sea salt.

It is said that the addictiveness of the Sicilian *frittura* comes from the recipe of the oil, which is in fact not really a recipe, more of a technique; the *friggatorias* never fully replace their old oil and only top it up with new when needed, not dissimilar to the *solera* system used in the making of sherries, vinegars, ports, Marsala and many spirits.

This may or may not be true (as is the Sicilian way) but there's no doubt it's hard to resist these fried, salty delights washed down with an ice-cold beer, watching the throng of Palermo street markets, hustle and bustle. If it wasn't so hot, you could imagine yourself in Skegness.

Fried Olives
with smoked mozzarella and dried chilli

These fantastic salty, smoky and crunchy olives are a staple bar snack in Sicily and around the mainland in Naples. They make the perfect drinking partner and are ideal when matched with an ice-cold bottle of Birra Moretti.

I also like to stuff these with a salty blue cheese such as gorgonzola and a little piece of sweet, fresh orange.

Serves 4

50g smoked mozzarella or
    scamorza cheese
½ teaspoon dried chilli flakes
12 large pitted green olives such
    as Nocellara, drained
50g plain flour

1 free-range egg, beaten
50g panko breadcrumbs
1 litre olive oil for frying
sea salt and freshly ground
    black pepper

Cut the mozzarella into 12 small pieces – small enough to be pushed into the olive cavity. Season each piece, then sprinkle with a little chilli. Stuff into the olives.

Roll each olive in flour, then dip in the egg and finally coat with breadcrumbs, ensuring they are completely coated.

Heat the oil in a deep pan to 170°C (a pinch of the breadcrumbs dropped in should fizzle straightaway).

Drop the olives into the hot oil and fry for 2–3 minutes or until golden brown. The cheese will have started to melt in the middle. Blot the olives on a kitchen towel, sprinkle with sea salt and serve as a snack.

Sardine Fritters
with alioli

Historically these sardine meatballs would have been a peasant replacement for expensive or unobtainable meat. However, such is their deliciousness that they have become a signature dish of Sicily in their own right.

I love the strong, almost bullying rich flavour of sardines. In this fantastic recipe their strong flavour is balanced with handfuls of fresh herbs, lemon, sweet raisins and a little kick of chilli.

More traditional versions call for the fritters to be cooked in a rich tomato sauce, but this is a more snacky version – deep fried and served with a cool, garlicky alioli for dipping.

Serves 4–6

15 fresh sardines, filleted and as many
    other bones removed as possible,
    or 4 x 120g cans of sardines
1 small onion, grated
100g fresh breadcrumbs
2 tablespoons plump raisins
3 tablespoons pine nuts
½ teaspoon dried chilli flakes
a handful of flat-leaf parsley
    leaves, chopped
a handful of mint leaves, chopped

2 tablespoons dry Marsala
2 teaspoons extra virgin olive oil
sea salt and freshly ground
    black pepper

To finish
about 1.5 litres groundnut oil
    for frying
juice of ½ lemon
alioli (see page 283)

Slice the fresh sardines into small pieces no bigger than 5mm. If using canned sardines, drain them and roughly mash with a fork. Mix the sardines with the rest of the ingredients.

Heat the groundnut oil in a deep-fat fryer or a deep saucepan to 170°C (a small piece of bread dropped in will fizzle and brown on contact with the oil).

Test the flavour of the mix by making just one fritter to begin with: take some of the mixture and shape with your hands into a small cake about 3cm across. Fry it in the hot oil until lightly golden brown on both sides and cooked through. Taste the fritter and adjust the seasoning of the remaining mixture if necessary, then shape the rest of the mix into 3cm cakes. You'll be able to make about 20.

Fry the fritters in 2 batches for 4–5 minutes or until golden brown and cooked through. Drain well on kitchen paper, then season well and add a squeeze of lemon juice. Serve with the alioli.

Asparagus Fritti
with lemon verbena

Wild asparagus is found growing all over the Sicilian countryside: a long, spindly and darker version of the more familiar thick, green-stemmed variety we enjoy in the spring in the UK. The wild variety has a more intense, bitter and peppery flavour and is very quick to cook or can even be eaten raw. A favourite way to cook asparagus in Sicily is to dip in a light batter, fry quickly and serve as an antipasto. I've matched it here with a an intriguingly fragrant salsa made with lemon verbena leaves.

Serves 4 as antipasti

400g very fresh asparagus
1.5 litres groundnut oil for frying

For the batter
200g plain flour, sifted
1 teaspoon baking powder
500ml cold sparkling water

For the salsa
a handful of lemon verbena, leaves picked
a handful of flat-leaf parsley leaves
20g capers
150ml extra virgin olive oil
1 salted anchovy
juice of 1 lemon
sea salt and freshly ground black pepper

First make the batter. Whisk together the flour, baking powder and chilled water. Leave to rest.

Meanwhile, make the lemon verbena salsa. Put the lemon verbena leaves, parsley, capers, olive oil, anchovy and some seasoning in a jug blender and pulse to form a coarse green sauce. Add a squeeze of lemon juice and pulse again. Check the seasoning and reserve.

Trim the woody ends from the asparagus. If very fresh the stalks won't need to be peeled.

Heat the oil in a deep-fat fryer or deep saucepan to about 170°C (a small amount of batter dropped into the oil will fizzle and turn golden brown straight away). Transfer the asparagus to the batter and turn to coat well, then one at a time drop the spears into the hot oil. (Don't overcrowd the pan – you may need to fry in 2 batches.) Deep-fry the asparagus until golden brown. Remove from the oil and drain well on kitchen paper. Season with sea salt and a little squeeze of lemon, and serve piping hot with the salsa for dipping.

Fried potatoes, pecorino cream and truffle

This Sicilian-inspired dish was created for Norma and is one of our most popular dishes. It's not really a dish that you are likely to find on the island of Sicily, but its origins are firmly rooted there. The potatoes are slowly fried in olive oil to crisp, and then mixed with a creamy sauce packed full of salty pecorino cheese and finished with a grating of seasonal truffle. I could happily eat a bowl of these just on their own, though they make for a great accompaniment to the roast chicken on page 200.

Serves 4

650g chipping potatoes (such as Maris Piper), peeled and cut into 1.5cm chunks
200ml double cream
100g pecorino cheese (or Parmesan), grated

1 tablespoon white truffle oil
1.5 litres olive oil
1 small black truffle
sea salt and freshly ground black pepper

Rinse the potatoes in cold water, then place in a pan of salted water. Bring to a simmer and par-cook – the potatoes should still be a little firm in the centre. Drain immediately and spread out the potatoes on a tray to cool for at least 1 hour.

Simmer the cream slowly in a saucepan over a low heat to reduce by about half. Whisk in two-thirds of the pecorino and the truffle oil and season well. Cook gently, still whisking, for 2–3 minutes or until the sauce is smooth. Set aside.

Heat the olive oil in a deep-fat fryer or deep saucepan to 160°C (a small piece of bread should fizzle immediately when dropped in).

Carefully transfer the potatoes to the oil and fry for about 8 minutes or until golden brown and crisp. Remove from the oil, drain well and season. Serve in a bowl with the sauce poured over the top, sprinkled with the remaining cheese and then some sliced truffle for a decadent finish.

Panelle

Panelle are one of the oldest and most popular of Palermo's street foods. These delicious flat fried chickpea flour cakes are Arabic in origin and have been made in pretty much the same way since the Middle Ages. They are wonderful when seasoned well and eaten fresh from the fryer with a surprising flavour from the gram flour.

I've eaten plenty of these walking around Palermo's street markets – some good and some pretty bad – and you will often see them stuffed into Sicilian sesame bread to make a hefty and filling sandwich. I prefer them unadorned with a tasty, cooling dip. Great for a snack or served as antipasti.

Serves 6

600ml water
250g chickpea flour
mixed vegetable oil and olive oil for
    deep-frying (⅔ vegetable oil and
    ⅓ olive oil)
1 tablespoon fennel seeds,
    lightly crushed

alioli (see page 283) or salsa verde
    (see page 280) to serve
sea salt and freshly ground
    black pepper

Bring the water to the boil in a saucepan and season well, then vigorously whisk in the chickpea flour a bit at a time to create a thick, smooth paste that comes away from the side of the pan. Check the seasoning again before removing from the heat.

Lightly oil a baking tray or your work surface and pour the chickpea paste on to this. Smooth out to a thickness of about 2cm. Leave to cool completely.

Heat the oil in a deep-fat fryer or deep saucepan to 180°C (a small piece of bread dropped in will fizzle and turn brown straight away).

Slice the chickpea paste into rustic strips or triangular shapes. Fry in 2 or 3 batches in the hot oil until golden brown, lightly puffed and crisp. Drain immediately on kitchen paper. Sprinkle with the fennel seeds and sea salt and serve immediately. I like to dip these, while still piping hot, in alioli or salsa verde.

Spaghettini Fritters
with Parmesan sauce

These fritters are incredibly delicious. They are a version of a Sicilian peasant dish that uses up leftover cooked pasta which is mixed with the last remnants of a meat sauce and then fried into a crispy snack. Gastronomic frugality at its most creative.

When I opened Norma, I decided to put this version on the snack menu and they proved an instant hit, selling hundreds of portions every week. The irony now is that we have to cook extra pasta and extra sauce in order to make them!

Serves 4

300g dried very fine spaghettini
extra virgin olive oil for dressing
 the pasta
200ml fresh chicken stock
30g butter
1 free-range egg, beaten
200g Parmesan cheese, grated

1.5 litres groundnut oil for frying
sea salt and freshly ground
 black pepper

For the Parmesan sauce
200ml double cream
100g Parmesan cheese, grated

Cook the spaghettini in boiling salted water according to the packet instructions; drain well. Toss the spaghettini with some extra virgin olive oil in a bowl. Set aside.

Bring the chicken stock to the boil in a saucepan and reduce by half. Whisk in the butter. Pour this over the cooked spaghettini and toss well to ensure all the pasta is coated. Now add the egg, half the Parmesan and some seasoning, mixing well again.

To shape the pasta into fritters, wind up some spaghettini with a fork into a spiral about 5cm in diameter. As each fritter is shaped, place on it on a large plate sprinkled with a little of the remaining Parmesan. You'll be able to make about 12 fritters.

When all the pasta fritters have been shaped and are in one layer on the plate, sprinkle with more Parmesan. Lay a piece of baking parchment on top and then another plate. Now place a weight such as a can of food on top to press down on the fritters. Chill in the fridge for at least 1½ hours to set.

To make the sauce, pour the cream into a saucepan and bring slowly to the boil, then simmer until reduced by a third. Whisk in the Parmesan, ensuring it melts completely and the sauce is smooth and creamy. Season well and keep warm.

Heat the groundnut oil in a deep-fat fryer or deep saucepan to about 170°C (a piece of bread dropped in should fizzle and brown straight away). Fry the fritters in 2 batches: carefully drop into the hot oil and fry until golden brown and crisp. Drain well on kitchen paper and sprinkle liberally with more Parmesan. Serve with a pot of the Parmesan sauce on the side for dipping.

Fried Squid
with dried chilli, capers, sesame and sage

I can think of few things nicer than super fresh, crispy fried squid. A simple ingredient simply prepared which sadly can so often go horribly wrong in the cooking. You want hot, tender squid in a super crunchy coating. In this recipe the soaking in milk gently tenderises the squid without softening it and creates an adhesive layer to which the flours stick. The little, crunchy North African dukkah-style dressing is something I discovered in Trapeni and is great with seafood.

I've suggested a dip for the squid, although the Sicilians would consider anything that might compromise the batter's crispiness a sacrilege – I think it's a risk worth taking.

Serves 4

500g prepared squid, tentacles and all
200ml milk
4 tablespoons cornflour
4 tablespoons plain flour
1 teaspoon salt
1.5 litres vegetable oil for frying
a small handful of sage, leaves picked
a handful of capers

1 teaspoon sesame seeds
1 dried pepperoncini chilli, crushed,
    or 1 teaspoon dried chilli flakes
olive oil
juice of ½ lemon
alioli (see page 283) to serve
sea salt flakes

Remove the tentacles from the squid and cut the tubes/bodies into thick 1cm rings and large triangles. Score the triangles with a criss-cross pattern. Put the pieces of squid and the tentacles into a bowl and cover with the milk. Cover the bowl and leave in the fridge for up to 8 hours (even half an hour is better than nothing).

When ready to cook, mix together the flours and salt in a bowl. Heat the vegetable oil in a deep-fat fryer or deep saucepan to 180°C (a pinch of flour will sizzle when it hits the oil). First fry the sage leaves: drop them into the hot oil and fry for 1 minute or until crisp. Remove from the oil and drain on kitchen paper.

Next, fry the capers in the oil for a minute until crisp; drain well on kitchen paper. Tip into a bowl and add the sage leaves, sesame seeds, crushed chilli, a little olive oil and the lemon juice. Mix together gently.

Drain the squid well and partially pat dry (you want some moisture left on the squid so the flour adheres). Drag through the flour and shake off the excess. Fry in batches for 1–2 minutes or until crisp and slightly golden. Lay the squid on kitchen paper and sprinkle with salt, then tip on to a plate and spoon over the sesame-chilli mix. Serve with alioli to dip.

Cauliflower, Parmesan and Anchovy Fritters

Cauliflower fritters are a Palermo street food classic from the *friggitore* – hot and salty from the fryer and finished with a squeeze of lemon juice. Delicious.

My version incorporates some umami into the batter with the addition of Parmesan and chopped anchovies, two flavours that work very well with cauliflower. Perfect served with a glass of dry Marsala for an aperitivo.

Serves 4

½ large leafy cauliflower, cut into
    florets and leaves thinly sliced
1.5–2 litres groundnut oil for frying

For the batter
50g plain flour
50g cornflour
30g Parmesan, finely grated

2 salted anchovies, finely chopped
zest of ½ unwaxed lemon
½ teaspoon cayenne pepper
1 large free-range egg
75ml cold sparkling water
sea salt and freshly ground
    black pepper

Cook the cauliflower florets and leaves in boiling salted water for 5 minutes or until tender. Drain well, refresh under cold water and then drain again.

To make the batter, mix the flours together in a bowl with the Parmesan, anchovies, lemon zest and cayenne pepper. Make a well in the centre and add the egg. Mix with a wooden spoon, gradually adding the fizzy water and drawing the flour into the centre, until you have a smooth, thick batter. Season well. Add the cauliflower florets and leaves and stir to coat.

Heat the oil in a deep-fat fryer or deep pan to 180°C (a cube of bread dropped in will brown in about 30 seconds). Drop heaped tablespoons of the battered cauliflower into the hot oil and fry for 2 minutes or until crisp and golden brown. Lift out with a spider or slotted spoon to a plate lined with kitchen paper to drain while you continue frying.

Sprinkle sea salt liberally over the fried cauliflower and serve with either my home-made alioli on page 283 or the pine nut and saffron sauce on page 286.

Crispy Courgette Flowers
filled with fresh crab, chilli and basil

During spring and early summer, courgette flowers are in abundance in the Sicilian food markets. They are now becoming more widely available in the UK too, which is a very good thing.

They flowers are very versatile and can be tossed through salads, lightly wilted in olive oil with a squeeze of lemon or added to a pizza, but I'm pretty sure the best way to enjoy them is to stuff them; they have the perfect cavity for filling with tangy goat's cheese, or ricotta drizzled with honey, or even a stronger, saltier blue cheese with a tangy grape must. In this recipe the flowers are stuffed Trapani-style with fresh crab, chilli, mascarpone and basil.

Serves 4

100g fresh white crab meat
50g brown crab meat
75g mascarpone
1 small, fresh red chilli, deseeded and finely chopped
8 large basil leaves, torn
lemon juice
8 courgette flowers with the stalk

2 litres groundnut oil
sea salt and freshly ground black pepper

For the batter
200g plain flour, sifted
1 teaspoon baking powder
500ml cold sparkling water

To make the batter, combine the sifted flour, baking powder and cold water in a bowl. Season well and whisk together until smooth. Set aside.

Next make the crab filling. Pick over the white crab meat to remove any bits of shell and cartilage, then squeeze out any excess liquid. Mix the white meat with the brown meat, the mascarpone, chilli and torn basil. Season well with salt, pepper and lemon juice.

If the stalks of the courgette flowers are thick, slice through the middle of the stalk lengthways to help speed the cooking process. Carefully open the petals and remove the stamen from each flower.

Now, divide the crab filling among the flowers, spooning the filling into the flower cavities. Lightly twist the petals to seal each flower and fold the twist under. Place the filled flowers, twist side down, on a tray and keep in the fridge until ready to fry.

Heat the oil in a deep-fat fryer or a deep saucepan to 170°C (a little batter dropped into the oil should fizzle and brown straight away).

Fry in 2 batches: dip each flower into the batter, ensuring it is fully coated, then carefully place in the hot oil – if you lower the head of the flower in first it seals in the filling. Fry the flowers for 2 minutes or so, turning them, until the batter is a light golden brown.

Drain the flowers on kitchen paper and season well. These are perfect as antipasti dipped into alioli (see page 283) or the pine nut and saffron sauce on page 286.

Saffron Arancini
with pork and veal ragù

No snack is more beloved in Sicily than these saffron-scented, ragù-filled rice balls. They are the complete package: rice, cheese and meat, all in one.

The origins of these arancini are clearly Arabic; the rice, the frying of course, but also the addition of saffron, adding a lovely yellow hue and aromatic flavour. In the Middle Ages saffron, abundant and cheap, was added to pretty much everything. The Parmesan here brings everything together perfectly. And I love the gooey stretch of melted mozzarella when the arancini are cut into. The best way to eat arancini and to enjoy the flavours to the full is warm, rather than piping hot.

Serves 6

For the saffron risotto
40g unsalted butter
1 shallot, finely chopped
240g Carnaroli rice
250ml white wine
2 pinches of saffron threads
about 1.25 litres chicken stock,
    preferably home-made
120g Parmesan cheese, grated
olive oil for cooking

For the ragù
extra virgin olive oil for cooking
1 garlic clove, chopped
250g minced pork
250g minced rose veal
250ml red wine

1 celery stick, finely chopped
1 small onion, finely chopped
1 carrot, finely chopped
20g butter
1 bay leaf
a pinch of grated nutmeg
700g canned chopped tomatoes

For the arancini
80g buffalo mozzarella cheese,
    cut into 12 pieces
2 eggs
panko breadcrumbs
about 2 litres vegetable oil for frying
sea salt and freshly ground
    black pepper

First prepare the saffron risotto. Place a deep-sided sauté pan over a medium heat and add the butter with the finely chopped shallot. Cook until translucent, then add the rice and stir to toast it slightly. Add the white wine and simmer until it has evaporated.

Add the saffron, then gradually stir in the chicken stock while simmering. Cook for 15–17 minutes in all. Remove the sauté pan from the heat and let it sit for a moment before mixing in the cheese. Season. Leave to cool to room temperature.

For the ragù, place a sauté pan over a high heat and add some olive oil, the garlic and the meat. When the meat begins to brown, add the red wine and simmer until it has evaporated. Once the meat is cooked through, remove from the heat and drain the meat in a sieve set over a bowl to catch the meat jus. Set aside.

...continued on page 68

In another sauté pan, cook the celery, onion and carrot in the butter over a medium heat until the vegetables are translucent. Add the bay leaf, nutmeg and cooked meat and mix in, then add the tomatoes and the meat jus. Turn the heat down to low and cook gently, covered, for at least 1½ hours. Remove from the heat and allow the ragù to cool to room temperature.

Add the saffron rice to the ragù and mix together. With your hands, form 12 cakes about the size of your palm out of the rice and ragù mixture. Insert a piece of mozzarella into the centre of each cake and mould it into a pear-shaped sphere.

Beat the eggs in a bowl and spread the breadcrumbs on a tray. Pass the arancini first through the eggs, coating them completely, and then into the breadcrumbs, pressing lightly so they adhere. Leave to set in the fridge for an hour before cooking.

Preheat the oven to 190°C/170°C fan/Gas Mark 5.

Heat the oil in a deep-fat fryer or deep saucepan to 170°C (a small piece of bread will fizzle and brown when dropped in). Carefully place the breadcrumbed arancini in the hot oil and fry until golden brown and crisp. Drain well on kitchen paper, then transfer to a baking tray and finish cooking in the oven for 10 minutes or until hot inside. Rest for 10 minutes to cool, then serve.

Spiced Lamb Arancini
with peas, broad beans and mint

Arancini – consisting of risotto rice which is shaped, filled and then deep fried to be given a second delicious life – are favoured snacks all over the islands. Traditionally the arancini are served warm or at room temperature as a street or bar snack, usually wrapped in greaseproof paper, to be eaten with a cold beer or on the hoof while tackling the markets. This version is perhaps slightly cheffy in that the arancini are smaller than usual and are served with a fresh, spring vegetable garnish. I like to serve these hot from the fryer too.

Here the rice isn't filled, but the spiced lamb mix is stirred through the rice as if a risotto. The spicing nods to the legacy left by the Moors during their occupation in the Middle Ages.

Makes about 12 (4 starter portions)

25g unsalted butter
200g arborio rice
500ml boiling chicken stock
olive oil for cooking
1 large onion, chopped
2 garlic cloves, crushed
250g minced lamb
1½ teaspoons ground allspice
2 teaspoons chopped dill
2 teaspoons chopped mint
30g Parmesan cheese, grated
40g thawed frozen peas,
    roughly chopped
about 50g plain flour

2 free-range eggs, lightly beaten
150g panko breadcrumbs
rapeseed oil for frying
sea salt and freshly ground
    black pepper

For the salad
50g thawed frozen peas
40g thawed frozen broad beans,
    grey 'jackets' peeled
a small handful each of dill and
    mint leaves
juice of ½ lemon
extra virgin olive oil

Melt the butter in a medium sauté pan. Add the rice and turn up the heat to high. Cook for 2 minutes, stirring constantly, then add 100ml of the stock and boil for 2 minutes. Turn down the heat. Gradually add the rest of the stock, stirring frequently, and simmer until all the stock has been absorbed and the rice is cooked al dente (if it needs more cooking after using up the stock, add some boiling water). This stage should take 40–45 minutes. Transfer the cooked rice to a bowl and set aside.

Heat a little olive oil in a sauté pan on a medium-high heat. Add the onion and garlic and cook, stirring occasionally, for 5 minutes or until the onion has softened. Add the lamb, ¾ teaspoon salt and a good grind of black pepper. Cook, stirring occasionally, for 5 minutes or until the lamb is cooked through.

Drain most of the oil from the pan (or transfer the meat mixture to a colander and leave to drain for a few minutes), then add the meat to the warm rice along with the allspice, dill,

...continued on page 70

mint, Parmesan and chopped peas. Season with more black pepper. Stir to mix, then with your hands shape the mixture into balls weighing about 50g each.

Put the flour, eggs and breadcrumbs in 3 separate bowls. Roll the rice-and-meat balls first in the flour, then in the egg and, finally, in the breadcrumbs so they're well coated.

Pour a 5mm depth of rapeseed oil into a large sauté pan and set on a medium-high heat. Once the oil is hot (test by dropping in a cube of bread: it should sizzle and turn golden and crisp in about 40 seconds), fry the balls in batches for 4–5 minutes, turning so they colour and crisp on all sides. Transfer to a kitchen paper-lined plate and keep warm until all the arancini are cooked.

To make the salad, stir together the peas, beans, dill and mint in a bowl and season well. Squeeze over the lemon juice and add a good lug of extra virgin olive oil.

Divide the arancini among the plates and spoon the spring salad on top.

pasta & rice

Though Naples is regularly offered up as the originator and epicentre of pasta in Italy, it was Sicily that set the pace and created this classic beloved Italian staple.

It was during the Roman occupation (241 BC–AD 476) that Sicily was first turned into what amounted to a giant wheat factory. The countryside was planted with plain upon plain of durum wheat to feed the hungry mainland. Later, under Arab occupation (837–902), and with profit in mind, the wheat production was commercialised via a clever mixture of smart growing strategies and sophisticated irrigation systems. Following harvest, the wheat was dried in the sun into a type of thin vermicelli noodle transforming it into something that we know now as pasta. An early documentation by al-Idrisi, the twelfth century Arab geographer, notes the semolina flour being shaped into long strands and dried out in the baking sun near the city of Palermo, ready for shipping off to the southern territories including Calabria and Puglia.

To this day, pasta in Sicily and on the surrounding islands is a loved staple, often eaten twice a day – the islanders are teasingly referred to as *mangiamacheroni*, the macaroni eaters!

To understand pasta in Italy you have to understand the north and the south. The north uses more fresh egg pasta and stuffed pasta such as raviolis, whilst in the south, and in particularly Sicily, pasta is made with durum wheat flour and water – no eggs – and the pasta is dried out before cooking. This difference is largely down to climate where the natural heat of the south allows the eggless pasta to be dried quickly and effectively. Heat is no friend to egg pasta, quickly both drying and cracking and becoming hard to work. However, egg pasta can be found in Sicily – I've eaten some excellent ricotta and wild fennel ravioli in Modica and elsewhere over the years – but it's the exception that proves the rule.

Dry straight pastas such as spaghetti are generally bought from the shops whilst at home the nonnas will make a dough, roll and twist into shapes, ready to be dried and then cooked. Which pasta is paired with what sauce is a relaxed affair in Sicily, unlike in the more rigid north where there are strict rules not to be broken!

It is the *timballo* and baked pastas that best typify Sicilian pasta glory – there is nothing quite like them (see the recipes throughout this chapter). During the fifteenth century, pasta changed from being a food of the poor and peasant class to the choice of the wealthy and the upper classes. This change manifested itself in audacious and luxurious pasta pies (*timballo*) that would be filled with anything and everything from tomatoes, herbs and vegetables to truffles, chicken livers and goat ragùs, which would sometimes, on high days and holidays, be encased in pastry or deep fried in breadcrumbs and pork fat. These Baroque dishes were served ceremoniously as a centrepiece for the table. *Timballo* live on and are still very popular on Sundays in the big cities and towns.

On a recent visit to the island I enjoyed a deliciously rich *timballo* that was layered with salty cheese, rice, eggs and squashed *polpette* meatballs. The *timballo* had been baked long and slowly so the cheese was gooey and melting, allowing a layer of breadcrumbs to form into a deep golden crust on top. It was brought to the table in style and with ceremony and proudly sliced into wedges – it was a showstopper.

You are quite likely to see these *timablli* and other pasta bakes if you go to the beach on a summer Sunday – it's the ideal picnic for Sicilian families who simply can't go without their daily pasta fix.

Each region in Sicily has its own signature pasta dish. Coastal regions focus on seafoods – Palermo has its pasta with sardines, raisins and pine nuts, while Messina has its swordfish and tomato ragùs with quadrucci pasta. I love the inland Sicilian ragùs; they are more fragrant and scented than their northern cousins. One of my favourite pasta dishes is a pork ragù flavoured with orange and mint (see page 112); it's a dish I created for Norma, inspired by sauces sampled on the west side of the island. Almonds feature heavily in pastas, either as a sauce such as an almond pesto (Trapanese style) or simply toasted or blended to a smooth purée sauce to coat spaghetti.

Sicilians like to use fried breadcrumbs in their pasta dishes – it is an eccentricity that I have now come to love. Indeed, they love breadcrumbs with pretty much everything savoury, which when added in the right quantities provides a crucial textural crunch.

But above all else, and not withstanding some of the many wonderful and lavishly executed celebratory preparations, the pasta dishes of Sicily and the islands are simple, fresh and vibrant, cooked with a love and passion for the ingredients that is uniquely Sicilian.

tips on making & cooking pasta

You can buy brilliant dried pasta (made using durum wheat and water) in all shapes and sizes and also fresh egg pasta too. However, if you fancy having a go yourself there are two recipes in the basics section of the book (see page 288 and 289), and below is a good method to follow for rolling out my dough recipes. This method applies to both egg and eggless dough, although you will find the egg dough softer. It is a lovely, easy and therapeutic task and there's nothing like your own fresh pasta – it's like the difference in buying and baking bread. (The ricotta ravioli recipe on page 92 will require homemade pasta, but all the other pasta recipes in this chapter can use shop-bought pasta.)

It is possible to make fresh pasta without a machine or mixer attachment but it's quite laborious and the results will be inconsistent – unless you have the lifelong skills of a Sicilian nonna who's rolled twice a day for a lifetime! I'd recommend buying a machine or a pasta rolling attachment for a food processor or mixer.

Pasta is best rolled out and worked with in a cool environment and on a cool surface such as marble, granite or stainless steel if possible. To roll out the pasta dough, first dust the counter with semolina flour and place the dough on top. Cut the dough in half and cover one piece with clingfilm and set aside.

Working with the remaining dough, lightly dust it with a little more semolina flour and press it down into a flat oval shape with your hands. With a counter-top pasta machine, or a pasta machine-attachment on your mixer, run the dough through the widest setting. Then fold the dough in three folds (like folding a letter) and run it again. Repeat once more.

Now you should have a rectangular/oval-shaped dough with sort of uneven ends. Feed the dough through the machine or attachment again, but this time, STOP MIDWAY. Then bring the two ends of the dough together, overlap them and pinch them lightly so they stick. Hold them in

position and start running it again through the machine. Once the 'seam' passes through the machine, you should have a connected, conveyor belt looking pasta sheet that passes through the machine. Keep running the machine to ensure that the seam/connection point is tightly merged together. Now, there is no more need to keep re-feeding.

All you have to do now is set the machine to the next notch, and keep the pasta sheet rolling through it (like a conveyor belt). Make sure to dust generously with semolina flour on top and underneath, and ensure that the entire length of the pasta sheet has passed through each increment before moving onto the next. Roll the pasta sheet out to your desired thickness, then sever it midway. Roll the pasta sheet out of the machine to release it and then cut into the desired shape. Repeat with the other half of the pasta dough.

cooking pasta

The first thing to remember about cooking pasta is to salt the water – you want a generous handful of table salt in the pan, around 8g of salt to a litre of water – and ensure there's plenty of water and it is boiling rapidly. Adding the pasta will lower the temperature so you want a fierce boil.

Cook the pasta to the packet instructions and to the required al dente degree. If you've made your own, then test a little first and time it until you are happy.

I always have my pasta sauce warm in a saucepan and then tip my cooked pasta, along with a little of the pasta water, into this. I'll then add some olive oil and toss through; this way the sauce coats all of the pasta. The pasta cooking water is very important; it's full of starch so it helps thicken the sauce and cling to the pasta. Due to the nature of pasta it cools down quickly and can become stodgy so serve it immediately and eat it quickly, as the Sicilians do!

rice

Though more of often associated with the north of Italy, rice has an important place in the Sicilian diet. And it is in arancini rather than risotto that Sicilians prefer their rice; those deep-fried golden balls of deliciousness filled with creamy rice and myriad stuffings of meat, fish and vegetables. Arancini are to be found lined up in the islands' fry shops and street food stalls, devoured as a supremely popular fast food.

Traditional arancini come in two main variants. The first, round in shape, is filled with a ragù sauce of meat, mozzarella and peas; the second, *al burro* (with butter), is made into a longer, pear-like shape, filled with diced mozzarella, prosciutto and grated cheese. The Sicilian city of Catania boasts two wonderful arancini, the *arancino alla Norma* made with aubergine and also a version made with Bronte pistachios. In other regions, the fillings might include mushrooms, sausage, gorgonzola, chicken, swordfish and even squid ink.

In the dessert section I have included the most delicious and unusual rice fritter recipe with orange blossom, a dish I found in a café in Marsala (see page 246). Its origins are clearly Arabic but somewhere along the line the rice has replaced what would have been a type of sweet brioche dough.

Pasta alla Norma

Pasta alla Norma has become the unofficial signature dish of Sicily. Originally created in the city of Catania around the same time as Vincenzo Bellini's romantic opera 'Norma', it is said that the pasta was created as a homage to the composer and to the opera. Another story tells of a talented home cook who served her creation to a group of gourmands and was duly christened at the table via the classic Sicilian compliment of *Chista e na vera Norma* ('this is a real Norma'). Whatever the truth, the dish became an instant classic and its fame spread around the world.

Serves 4

2 firm aubergines, trimmed and cut into 2cm dice
150ml extra virgin olive oil
½ onion, finely chopped
2 garlic cloves, finely chopped
a good handful of basil leaves

800g quality canned chopped tomatoes or passata
400g dried rigatoni
200g ricotta salata cheese, grated
sea salt

Put the diced aubergines in a colander in the sink and sprinkle with salt. Leave to drain for 30 minutes.

Preheat the oven to its highest temperature, around 250°C/230°C fan/Gas Mark 10.

Rinse the aubergine in cold water and pat dry with a kitchen towel, then toss in a bowl with half the oil. Spread out on a baking tray, place in the oven and cook for 15–20 minutes or until caramelised, turning occasionally to make sure the pieces don't dry out.

Meanwhile, heat the remaining oil in a medium saucepan over a medium heat and add the onion and garlic. Sauté for a couple of minutes, then add half the basil and the tomatoes. Bring to a simmer. Turn down the heat and cook gently for 23–30 minutes or until thickened (the exact time will depend on your canned tomato brand).

When the sauce is almost ready, cook the pasta in plenty of boiling salted water according to the packet instructions to al dente. Add the aubergine to the sauce. Drain the pasta (reserving a little of the cooking water) and toss in the sauce. If the sauce seems too thick, add some cooking water to loosen.

Divide among the plates and sprinkle with the ricotta and remaining basil leaves, roughly torn over the top. It's best to allow this to cool slightly before eating.

Pasta with Lemon, Sage, Chilli and Parmesan

I love this pasta recipe. It's a Sicilian classic, little known outside of the island. Lemon is the star of the show and everything else the talented supporting cast.

The addition of butter isn't the traditional Sicilian way and by including it I am risking life and limb. The Sicilians would use lots of olive oil, but I think the addition of butter gives the sauce a lovely velvety texture and gently tempers the mouth-puckering acidity of the citrus. Use the very best fruits available to you, unwaxed and full of lemony character.

Serves 4

extra virgin olive oil for cooking
40g fine dried breadcrumbs
50g unsalted butter
1 fresh red chilli, deseeded and
    finely chopped
1 garlic clove, finely sliced
1 salted anchovy, chopped
zest and juice of 1 large
    unwaxed lemon

120g Parmesan cheese, grated
a handful of sage leaves
400g dried spaghetti, linguine
    or bucatini
sea salt and freshly ground
    black pepper

Heat a little oil in a small sauté pan and gently fry the breadcrumbs until they start to turn a light golden brown. Drain and reserve.

Add a lug of olive oil to a medium sauté pan set over a medium heat, then add the butter. When the butter starts to bubble gently and foam (not brown), stir in the chilli, garlic and anchovy. Cook for a minute. Add the lemon zest and juice. Remove from the heat. Add the Parmesan and sage and stir well. Keep warm.

Cook the pasta in boiling salted water according to the packet instructions. Drain, reserving some of the pasta cooking water.

Transfer the pasta to the buttery lemon sauce along with a lug of pasta water. Return to the heat and toss the pasta with the sauce using a spoon or tongs, ensuring that all the pasta is coated and the sauce is rich and reduced. Season with a little more salt and black pepper, then serve immediately sprinkled with the breadcrumbs.

Spaccatelle
with ricotta and green pistachio pesto

This pasta dish is very much about the pistachios. Try to find the freshest most green nuts you can – the Sicilian Bronte pistachios are delicious as are some Iranian varieties. The lime is an unusual addition but completely works with nuts. This pesto recipe makes about double that which you need so store it in the fridge and use it with everything, from pasta to fish and from meats to vegetables.

I've used spaccatelle here, a traditional dried pasta that's mostly found in southern Italian and Sicilian pasta dishes and can be sourced from most of the big pasta brands such as Barilla and Dececco.

Serves 4 as primi

400g dried spaccatelle
extra virgin olive oil
a handful of grated Parmesan cheese
100g fresh sheep's ricotta, plus extra
   to finish

For the pistachio pesto
50g basil leaves
100g flat-leaf parsley, leaves picked

1 small garlic clove, peeled
6 heaped tablespoons shelled
   pistachios (very green Iranian nuts
   are best), plus extra to finish
zest of 1 lime
4 teaspoons lime juice
250ml extra virgin olive oil
sea salt and freshly ground
   black pepper

To make the pesto, blitz everything together in a blender and season well.

Cook the pasta in boiling salted water according to the packet instructions. Drain, reserving some of the pasta cooking water, and tip back into the pan. Add a good lug of olive oil, a ladle of pasta water and then the Parmesan and pesto. Toss through, ensuring the pasta is coated well and there's a good sauce consistency.

Remove from the heat, stir in the ricotta and toss a couple of times. Finish with a sprinkle of extra pistachios and ricotta if desired, then serve immediately.

Baked Conchiglioni
with pumpkin and rosemary

As with many Sicilian recipes these stuffed pasta shells are born from need and ingenuity, making the best use of leftovers – pasta in this case. The resulting dish has become something much more than the sum of its parts and is a real showstopper. Conchiglioni is the most popular stuffing pasta in Sicily though lumaconi, snail shell shapes, are also good for stuffing and look great.

Although there are several elements to this recipe it's easy to prepare. I've taken it up a notch with the addition of mascarpone in the sauce and an indulgent rosemary and lemon spiked brown butter to finish.

Serves 4

about 1kg dense-fleshed pumpkin or
    butternut squash, peeled, deseeded
    and cut into 2cm dice
olive oil for cooking
a handful of baby spinach, chopped
400g dried large conchiglioni
    (pasta shells)
250g unsalted butter

150g plain flour
700ml full-fat milk
125g mascarpone
80g fontina cheese, finely grated
4 sprigs of rosemary, leaves picked
juice of ½ lemon
sea salt and freshly ground
    black pepper

Preheat the oven to 200°C/180°C fan/Gas Mark 6. Spread the pumpkin dice on a roasting tray, season well and drizzle with oil. Roast for 25–30 minutes or until the pumpkin is tender and has started to brown. Remove from the oven and crush with the back of a wooden spoon or a fork, then stir in the chopped baby spinach to wilt in the residual heat. Reserve. Leave the oven on.

While the pumpkin is cooking, partly cook the pasta in boiling salted water for 5 minutes. Drain and refresh under cold running water to stop any further cooking. Drain again.

Make the béchamel by melting 125g of the butter in a saucepan and stirring in the flour. Turn up the heat and cook until this roux bubbles and turns a sandy colour. Now gradually whisk in the milk, still on the heat, and continue to whisk until the milk is fully incorporated and the sauce is smooth and thick but pourable. Stir in the mascarpone and 40g of the fontina and season to taste. Spoon the béchamel into a large baking dish and drizzle with olive oil.

Divide the pumpkin mix among the pasta shells and push it in – it's easiest to use your finger. You should over-stuff them so you can see plenty of filling. Press the pasta shells into the béchamel in rows. Drizzle with more oil, then bake for 30 minutes. Remove from the oven and sprinkle with the remaining fontina. Place back in the oven and bake until the shells are fully cooked and the top is golden brown.

While the pasta is baking, heat the remaining butter in a saucepan and cook over a medium heat until it turns a nut brown or 'noisette'. Add the rosemary leaves, lemon juice and seasoning. Remove the pasta bake from the oven and cool for 5 minutes before spooning over the brown rosemary butter and serving.

Ricotta, Parmesan and Lemon Ravioli
with wild garlic

Ricotta ravioli can be enjoyed in many Sicilian restaurants, often served with a lemon or tomato sauce. My version includes an egg yolk popped into the centre of the ravioli that stays soft through the cooking creating a lovely eggy sauce inside the pasta. The naturally bland ricotta is given a flavour boost by the addition of lemon, Parmesan and nutmeg.

I love wild garlic which I'm pleased to see is becoming ever more present in the British countryside in early spring. If wild garlic is unavailable, then substitute baby spinach and a little chopped garlic.

Ravioli are not difficult to make, just get well organised and make sure you have everything to hand before you begin.

Serves 6

70g Parmesan cheese, grated, plus
   extra to serve
100g ricotta cheese, drained
nutmeg for grating
zest and juice of 1 unwaxed lemon
½ quantity of fresh egg pasta dough
   (see page 289)
6 medium free-range eggs

fine semolina for storing the ravioli
100g unsalted butter
a large handful of wild garlic leaves
   (or, if not available, a large handful
   of baby spinach and 1 finely chopped
   garlic clove)
sea salt and freshly ground
   black pepper

First, beat 50g of the Parmesan with the ricotta, then season with salt and pepper, 3 gratings of nutmeg and half of the lemon zest. Spoon into a piping bag and leave in the fridge while you roll out your dough.

Divide the dough in half and roll out each piece into a sheet, following the instructions for rolling out the pasta on page 289 and taking the pasta to about 1mm thickness.

Lay the pasta sheets on a clean surface. Starting 2.5cm away from the long edge of one pasta sheet, carefully pipe a ring of the ricotta mixture about 5cm in diameter on to the pasta.

Separate an egg and carefully drop the yolk into the middle of the ricotta circle – it should fit snugly. Pipe your next ring of ricotta on the pasta sheet 5cm away from your first one, then gently drop in an egg yolk. Continue like this to make 4 more yolk-filled rings. (Keep the egg whites for another dish.)

Brush the exposed pasta with water, then carefully lay the second sheet of pasta over the top.

Starting at one end, gently press the pasta around the outside of the filling, pushing out the air and sealing the edges. Using a 10cm round cutter, cut out a round raviolo with the egg right in the middle.

Check that the edges of the ravioli are sealed – use a little more water to help, if needed. As they are made, place the ravioli on a large tray dusted with the fine semolina, making sure they don't touch each other.

Bring a large pan of salted water to the boil, then reduce the heat to a rolling simmer. Carefully lower in the ravioli, 2 or 3 at a time, and cook for 4 minutes or until they float to the surface.

While cooking the ravioli, melt the butter in a medium sauté pan over a medium heat. As soon as it starts to foams, add the remaining lemon zest and a squeeze of juice. Season well.

Remove the pasta with a slotted spoon and place straight into the butter sauce, adding a splash of the pasta cooking water and the remaining Parmesan. Cook the next batch of ravioli, then add to the sauce.

With the heat still low, add the wild garlic leaves (or spinach and garlic) and carefully stir in to wilt – be careful not to break the ravioli.

Spoon the ravioli on to a serving dish and spoon over the wilted wild garlic (or spinach), then pour over the sauce and serve with extra Parmesan.

Rice Timballo

with tomatoes, marjoram and aubergine fritti

The *timballo* is one of those dishes that perfectly encapsulates Sicily's vibrant food culture; leftover risotto rice mixed with whatever's left around, which when baked into a 'pie' with a gleaming golden crust and then unmoulded with great ceremony at the table becomes a centrepiece as splendiferous as a prized roasted rib of beef. It might even earn a round of applause from the eagerly awaiting hungry diners…

My version is relatively simple and you could easily add your own spin – perhaps basil, courgettes, roasted peppers, fennel or a layer or two of a thick meat ragù.

Serves 6

1 small white onion, diced
1 garlic clove, finely chopped
olive oil
500g canned chopped tomatoes
1 tablespoon tomato paste
a handful of marjoram leaves
600g Carnaroli rice
2 aubergines
50g unsalted butter, softened

a handful of dried breadcrumbs for
   the mould
80g Parmesan cheese, finely grated
1 large free-range egg
250g provolone or mozzarella cheese,
   cut into small dice
sea salt and freshly ground
   black pepper

In a large sauté pan fry the onion and garlic in olive oil until soft but without colour. Add the tomatoes, tomato paste and marjoram. Simmer, stirring occasionally, for 30 minutes or until rich and thick.

Meanwhile, cook the rice in boiling salted water until just al dente. Drain and add to the tomato sauce. Cook for another few minutes, then season well to taste.

Cut one aubergine lengthways into 3mm-thick slices and the other aubergine into 1cm cubes. Set a large sauté pan over a medium heat and add plenty of olive oil. Firstly, fry the aubergine slices until golden brown on both sides. Remove to kitchen paper to drain. Now season and fry the diced aubergine until cooked through and golden brown. Drain well.

Preheat the oven to 200°C/180°C fan/Gas Mark 6. Butter a 20–23cm springform cake tin, or a timballo mould, and coat with breadcrumbs. Use the slices of aubergine to line the tin.

Add most of the Parmesan and the egg to the rice. Mix well, then press half of it on to the aubergine lining the bottom of the tin. Cover with a layer of half the aubergine cubes, then a layer of about half of the cheese cubes. Add another layer of aubergine cubes and cover with the rest of the rice mix, pressing down firmly. Finish with the remaining cheese cubes and the last of the Parmesan.

Bake for 25 minutes. Remove from the oven and leave to cool for 10 minutes, then run a knife around the inside edge of the tin to loosen the timballo. Unclip the side of the tin and transfer the timballo to a plate.

Lemon, Parmesan, Chilli and Basil Linguine

This is one of the simplest of pasta dishes and when the very best lemons are to hand, it sparkles. The lemons are the basis for the sauce so go for a knobbly unwaxed variety for maximum flavour. In January and February, when the enormous lemons from Sicily and the Amalfi coast arrive, I'll cook this dish once or twice a week. It never fails to surprise me how much flavour you can get into a pasta dish with so little input, but this is often the Sicilian way.

Serves 4

500g dried linguine
3 unwaxed Sicilian lemons
1 large, fresh red chilli, deseeded
    and chopped
about 100ml extra virgin olive oil

125g Parmesan cheese
a handful of basil, leaves picked
    and torn
sea salt and freshly ground
    black pepper

Cook the linguine in a pan of boiling salted water according to the packet instructions, then drain and return to the pan.

While the pasta is cooking, finely grate the zest from 1 lemon into a bowl. Squeeze the juice from all 3 lemons and add to the bowl with the chilli. Slowly pour in the olive oil while whisking. Finely grate the Parmesan into the bowl, then beat everything together – the lemony sauce will turn creamy and emulsify. Season to taste and add extra lemon juice, if needed.

Add the lemony sauce to the hot drained linguine and toss in the pan to coat each strand of pasta (the Parmesan will slowly melt when mixed with the pasta). Add the basil. Serve immediately.

Pasta Braised with Kale, Tomato Cruda and Pecornio

This is my version of the Palermo classic *pasta con i tenurumi* which is a delicious seasonal dish more soup-like than a traditional pasta dish, and not unlike a minestrone. This version has more pasta than soup and I like to stir in a raw tomato mix instead of a tinned tomato sauce making the finished dish much fresher.

Tenurumi translates as 'tender' in the Sicilian dialect and refers to the long tendril-like leaves of the cucuzza courgette, a variety specific to the island and in season all through the hot dry summer. A specialist grocer could help you help source it but there are some delicious slightly bitter kales or chards which would make perfect alternatives. Cooking the pasta in the vegetable cooking water is a canny and typically creative Sicilian technique to maximise flavour.

Serves 4

6 medium-sized ripe vine tomatoes, 'eyes' removed and finely chopped
a handful of flat-leaf parsley leaves, chopped
2 garlic cloves, finely chopped
1 tablespoon red wine vinegar
extra virgin olive oil
1 small courgette, cut in half lengthways, deseeded and sliced

400g kale (such as cavolo nero, or tenerumi if you can get it), washed and chopped
200g dried spaghetti, broken into small pieces
60g pecorino or Parmesan cheese
sea salt and freshly ground black pepper

Place the chopped tomatoes in a bowl. Stir in the parsley, garlic and vinegar and pour over olive oil to cover. Season and reserve.

Bring a pan of salted water to the boil – you'll need around 1 litre. Plunge the courgette and kale into the water and cook for 2–3 minutes or until just tender. Remove the vegetables to a bowl, then cook the pasta in the same water according to the packet instructions.

A minute or so before the pasta has finished cooking, add the vegetables to the pot and stir through. Season well. Once the pasta is cooked, divide it and the vegetables among serving bowls, pouring in as much of the cooking liquid as you like. Stir in the marinated tomatoes, grate over the cheese and drizzle with extra virgin olive oil.

Spaghetti with Almond Cream, Fresh Crab, Chilli and Marjoram

Nut-thickened sauces and 'creams' are very popular in parts of Sicily. Nuts are natural thickeners and packed with flavour.

I first came across a pasta dish similar to this when traveling through the Aeolian islands one summer. An idyllic beach side café had just a couple of pasta options and the one that took my fancy was a spaghetti with almond sauce served with tiny wild mussels that were an ocean in every bite. I think there may have been lemon too. It couldn't have been more idyllic for the time and place. This is my version.

Serves 4

100g blanched almonds
300ml full-fat milk
400g dried spaghetti
extra virgin olive oil for cooking
2 fresh red chillies, deseeded and
 finely chopped
50g brown crab meat

100g fresh white crab meat, picked
 over to remove any shell or cartilage
juice of 1 lemon
a handful of marjoram leaves
sea salt and freshly ground
 black pepper

Put the almonds and milk in a saucepan and set aside to soak for 30 minutes. Then bring to the boil and cook for 5 minutes. Pour into a blender and blitz to a smooth sauce consistency. Season and reserve.

Cook the pasta in boiling salted water according to the packet instructions.

Meanwhile, add a lug of oil to a large sauté pan and gently heat, then add the chillies and fry lightly to soften. Now pour in the almond sauce and stir in the brown and white crab meat. Squeeze in some lemon juice and check the seasoning.

When the pasta is cooked, transfer it to the almond sauce using tongs. Drizzle in some olive oil and add a ladle of the pasta water.

Stir the pasta through with the tongs, ensuring the strands are all coated. If the sauce is too thick add more pasta water and continue to stir or toss through.

Transfer the pasta to warmed bowls (doing this with tongs gives a neat presentation) and sprinkle over the marjoram, then serve immediately.

Squid Ink, Squid, Chilli and Basil Linguine

Squid ink is divisive; the fact it is pitch black puts some people off trying it. It is, though, quite delicious. The rich creamy texture and briny, umami-laden flavours make it unique and very special. Ink pasta or *Pasta al nero* is a classic – I make a beeline for the seafood institution Colapesce just south of Syracuse where they make a sublime version of this, albeit with parsley instead of the basil that I've used here. The ink is available in little sachets from good fishmongers sold alongside the fresh squid. The only downside from eating this dish is the resulting goth look of black teeth and lips.

Serves 4

600g fresh squid, prepared, with tentacles
60ml extra virgin olive oil
3 garlic cloves (peeled)
100ml dry white wine
200g canned chopped tomatoes
1 fresh red chilli, finely chopped

400g dried linguine
an 8g sachet squid ink
2 tablespoons warm water
a handful of basil leaves
zest of 1 unwaxed lemon
sea salt and freshly ground black pepper

Cut the squid tubes/bodies into thin strips. Pour the oil into a large saucepan set over a medium heat. Add the garlic and allow it to infuse in the oil for 2 minutes.

Discard the garlic and add the squid. Sauté for 2 minutes or until just opaque, then pour in the wine. Boil to reduce by half before adding the chopped tomatoes and chilli. Lower the heat, cover and cook for about 20 minutes or until thick and rich.

Next, bring a large pot of salted water to the boil and plunge in the linguine. Cook according to the packet instructions.

While the pasta is cooking, dissolve the squid ink in the warm water and add to the squid sauce. Stir so the ink evenly colours the sauce black.

When the pasta is cooked, transfer to the sauce along with a ladle of the pasta cooking water and toss to coat the pasta strands. Throw in the basil and lemon zest and toss again, then serve.

Trapani-style Cus Cus

Trapani lies on the wild west coast of Sicily, just a few kilometres from mainland Tunisia in North Africa. It's here that the intertwining of the two food cultures of Sicily is perhaps most evident, joyously embraced by the town's weather-beaten fisherman. This hearty seafood stew gives a nod to the bouillabaisse of Marseille with layers of seductively aromatic flavours combining with an intensely rich stock in which basks a sparkling collection of locally caught fish. It is served with couscous, which is essentially semolina – itself a product of durum wheat, which was developed in Sicily during the Moorish occupation and then taken back across the sea to North Africa where it became a staple of Arab cuisine. On the western side of the island couscous remains highly popular and is celebrated with an annual festival.

A version of this dish can be found in my book *Moorish* – this version is simpler to make yet equally delicious. I love the almond, chilli and pistachio paste that is added at the end. I have Giovanni, one of my chefs from Norma, to thank for this dish and I'm sure his mum will be very happy to see it here in all its Trapani glory.

Serves 4

1.5kg fish on the bone (sea bream, red or grey mullet, bass or hake)
1 onion, finely chopped
1 celery stick, finely chopped
1 fennel bulb, finely sliced
a small bunch of flat-leaf parsley, leaves picked and stalks kept
½ teaspoon dried chilli flakes
olive oil for cooking
400g canned chopped tomatoes
4 bay leaves
2 litres water
350g couscous, rinsed
300g mixed prepared squid, debearded mussels and clams

200ml dry Marsala
lemon wedges for serving
sea salt and freshly ground black pepper

For the paste
3 garlic cloves, peeled
50g blanched almonds
50g pistachios
1 fresh red chilli, stalk end removed
a pinch of dried chilli flakes
50ml extra virgin olive oil

Ask a fishmonger to fillet the fish for you, reserving all the bones, heads etc. Cut the fillets into bite-sized pieces and set aside.

Heat a large deep sauté pan over a medium-high heat and fry the onion, celery and fennel with the parsley stalks and chilli flakes in a good lug of olive oil until they have softened but not coloured. Add the tomatoes and 2 of the bay leaves and cook for a minute or so, then add the water. Bring to the boil. Reduce to a simmer and add the fish bones, heads and any scraps to the pan. Simmer the stock, partially covered, for 40 minutes, then strain into a large pan. Season to taste and reserve.

...continued on page 108

To make the paste, blitz the garlic, almonds, pistachios, most of the parsley leaves, the fresh chilli and flakes, olive oil and a good pinch of salt into a paste. Add half of the paste to the fish stock, reserving the rest for serving later.

Place the remaining 2 bay leaves on the bottom of a warmed large, shallow serving bowl. Tip in the dry couscous. Pour over about 500ml of the fish stock. Cover with clingfilm and leave in a warm spot for 20 minutes.

Meanwhile, heat a little olive oil in a frying pan and fry the squid, mussels and clams for a few minutes or until the squid is just cooked through and the clams and mussels have opened. Turn up the heat, add the Marsala and boil quickly to evaporate. Cover with just enough fish stock to poach the fish. Add the pieces of fish to the pan, reduce to a simmer and cook for 10 minutes or so.

Fluff up the couscous with a fork. Ladle the fish and its cooking liquor over the couscous. Finish with a spoonful of the nut-chilli paste, the remaining parsley leaves and the lemon wedges. You can serve extra fish stock and the nut-chilli paste on the side to be passed around for those who want it.

Baked Sicilian Anelletti Timballo

Anelletti are little pasta rings that are very popular in Sicily, often baked into a *timballo*. Versions of *anelletti* can be found in bars, restaurant or fast food spots all over Palermo, perhaps with the addition of hardboiled eggs, slices of fried aubergines or different cheeses. Sicilians will find the time to make *anelletti* at home for a special occasion or a feast day. The result is often spectacular!

Serves 6

For the meat sauce
2 carrots, finely chopped
1 onion, finely chopped
3 garlic cloves, finely chopped
2 celery sticks, finely chopped
extra virgin olive oil
200g minced beef
200g minced pork
100ml red wine
350g tomato passata
a handful of basil leaves
150g thawed frozen peas

For the timballo
400g dried anelletti (little pasta rings)
3 tablespoons extra virgin olive oil
a handful of panko breadcrumbs,
    as required
150g cooked ham, cut into cubes
150g caciocavallo or pecorino
    cheese, grated
50g Parmesan cheese, grated
sea salt and freshly ground
    black pepper

First make the meat sauce. Sweat the carrots, onion, garlic and celery in olive oil until they start to soften but do not colour, about 10 minutes. Add the minced meat and cook until browned.

Add the red wine and stir well, then boil until the wine has evaporated. Pour in the passata and mix it in with the meat. Add the basil and season well. Cover the pan and simmer the meat sauce on a low heat for at least 1 hour, stirring occasionally so it doesn't stick. If it gets too thick add some water. About 10 minutes before the sauce has finished cooking, stir in the peas.

While the sauce is cooking you can get on with the rest of the dish. Put water on to boil for the pasta. Add salt once it starts to boil, then cook the pasta for 3 minutes less than the packet instructions. Drain the pasta well and toss with a drizzle of oil, then add to the meat sauce. Mix the pasta and sauce together and allow to cool.

Preheat the oven to 210°C/190°C fan/Gas Mark 6/7. Grease a 20–23cm non-stick springform cake tin, or the equivalent timballo tin for authenticity, with extra virgin olive oil. Coat the oiled tin with breadcrumbs.

Spoon a thick layer of the pasta and meat mixture, about half of it, into the tin to cover the bottom. Make a layer of the chopped ham and caciocavallo or pecorino cheese on this and finish off with another thick layer of the remaining pasta and meat sauce. Press the mixture down and cover the top with breadcrumbs and grated Parmesan. Bake for 30 minutes.

Remove the timballo from the oven and leave to cool for 15 minutes before removing from the tin to a serving plate. Serve with my Chilled Green Beans, Toasted Almonds, Shallots, Raisins and Orange on page 130.

Pork, Orange and Mint Ragù
with fusilli

This is certainly not an authentic Sicilian pasta dish, but I think it evokes perfectly the heady flavours of the island and its proud Arabic heritage – subtle scents of orange, mint and cinnamon underlying the rich pork ragù finished with pecorino.

This dish was on the opening menu of Norma and whilst it raised a few eyebrows from the pasta traditionalists it was an immediate success and became one of our most popular dishes. I'm a great believer in making meat ragùs the day before, leaving them to settle and rest overnight. This time spent does wondrous things to the flavours.

Serves 4

200g minced pork with a good
    amount of fat
50g pancetta or guanciale, finely diced
extra virgin olive oil for cooking
1 onion, finely chopped
2 garlic cloves, finely chopped
2 bay leaves
2 salted anchovies, finely chopped
500ml red wine
zest and juice of 1 large orange

500ml tomato passata
1 cinnamon stick
100ml water
400g dried fusilli (pasta spirals)
    or strozzapreti
pecorino or Parmesan cheese
    for grating
a handful of mint leaves
sea salt and freshly ground
    black pepper

Preheat the oven to 220°C/200°C/Gas Mark 7.

Lay the mince and pancetta or guanciale in a roasting tin, season and drizzle with oil. Cook in the oven for 25 minutes or until the meat is cooked through and has caramelised.

Meanwhile, heat some olive oil in a medium saucepan over a medium heat. Add the onion, garlic, bay leaves and anchovies and cook slowly to soften but not colour.

Remove the meat from the oven and add to the saucepan. Pour the wine and orange juice into the roasting tin and set this over a high heat. Boil while scraping the tin to deglaze and release all the meaty sediment. Now pour this into the saucepan.

Set the saucepan over a medium heat and boil the wine/juice to reduce to a syrup. Add the passata, cinnamon and water and stir well. Leave to simmer for 1 hour or until a thick and rich ragù consistency. Stir once in a while to prevent any sticking. Season well and stir in the orange zest.

Cook the pasta in boiling salted water according to the packet instructions. Lift out into the ragù. Drizzle with some oil and grate in some cheese. Add half the mint. Toss everything together, adding some of the pasta cooking water to loosen.

Immediately divide among serving bowls. Scatter the remaining mint on top and serve with extra grated cheese, if you like.

Pasta al Forno

with tomato, fennel sausage and red wine

This delicious *ragu al forno* is good with any dried short pasta that you might have in the cupboard, such as pennete, orecchiette or paccheri. You can find pork and fennel sausages in Italian delis or at good butchers.

Equally good served either at room temperature or piping hot from the oven.

Serves 4

extra virgin olive oil
4 quality large, plump pork and fennel
    sausages, skins removed and meat
    roughly chopped
250ml quality red wine (I used a Nero)
100ml water
200g ripe cherry tomatoes,
    cut into quarters
200g canned chopped tomatoes

150g purple sprouting broccoli,
    chopped
75g pecorino cheese, grated
500g dried short pasta (pennette,
    orecchiette or paccheri)
100g mascarpone
100g dried breadcrumbs
sea salt and freshly ground
    black pepper

Preheat the oven to 200°C/180°C fan/Gas Mark 6.

Heat a good lug of oil in a large sauté pan. Add the sausage meat and cook, stirring, for a few minutes to brown well. Pour in the wine. Scrape the bottom of the pan to deglaze and boil to reduce the wine down by three-quarters. Now add the water and the fresh and canned tomatoes. Cook for a few minutes to break up the tomatoes and reduce to a rich sauce. Add the broccoli and cook for a further 2 minutes, then throw in half the pecorino, season well and stir in.

Cook the pasta in boiling salted water according to the packet instructions. When cooked, add a ladle of the pasta water to the sauce, then drain the pasta (reserving some more of the liquid) and transfer to the sauce. Add some olive oil and toss the pasta through the sauce, ensuring it is well coated. You can add a little more pasta water if the sauce is too dry.

Turn the pasta out into a baking dish. Drizzle with more olive oil and sprinkle over the remaining pecorino. Spoon around the mascarpone. Finally, sprinkle over the breadcrumbs. Bake for 25–30 minutes or until piping hot and bubbling with a golden brown crust.

Goat Ragù and Busiate

In the UK goat has become an ever more popular choice in recent years, largely due to the efforts of Cabrito, a sustainable business selling kid goats which was born out of a problem of what to do with redundant dairy goats. In other parts of Europe goat is eaten as regularly as lamb or beef, where its tasty, healthy meat is highly appreciated. Younger goats have a flavour similar to that of a well-flavoured lamb or hogget, whilst older goats have a much earthier, gamey flavour.

Agrigento is the main goat region in Sicily and is the inspiration for this fantastic recipe – rosemary and lemon zest being a typical addition and busiate the pasta of choice. Either young or old goats would work here – I've tried them both.

Serves 4

extra virgin olive oil
1 small onion, finely chopped
2 garlic cloves, finely chopped
1 large carrot, finely chopped
1 bay leaf
200g minced kid goat shoulder (or lamb)
100g minced pork shoulder
30g diced pancetta
1 teaspoon tomato paste
⅔ bottle of gutsy red wine

400g quality canned chopped tomatoes
pared peel of ½ unwaxed lemon
1 teaspoon rosemary leaves
a little sherry or balsamic vinegar
100g Parmesan cheese, grated
about 400g dried busiate (long spiralled macaroni)
sea salt and freshly ground black pepper

Heat a large pan over a medium heat and add a lug of oil followed by the onion, garlic, carrot and bay leaf. Cook to soften without colouring. Now turn up the heat and add the minced meat and pancetta. Cook briskly to caramelise and cook through, stirring continually to make sure the mince is broken up and not clumped together.

Spoon in the tomato paste and stir, then pour over the red wine and bring to the boil. Turn down the heat and simmer until the wine has all but evaporated. Add the tomatoes, lemon zest, rosemary and a splash of water. Season with salt, pepper and a little vinegar to sharpen. Simmer for 30 minutes or until thick and rich.

Stir in half the Parmesan and 1 tablespoon of extra virgin olive oil. Cook for 10 minutes. Remove from the heat, cover and leave to rest for at least 30 minutes.

Bring a large pan of salted water to the boil over a high heat. Plunge in the pasta and cook according to the packet instructions until al dente. About 2 minutes before the pasta is ready, gently heat the ragù.

Drain the pasta, reserving some of the pasta water. Add the pasta and a couple of tablespoons of the cooking water to the ragù and toss well, ensuring the pasta is coated with the rich sauce and is not too dry. Add a little more pasta cooking water if necessary.

Divide the pasta among the plates and finish with more olive oil and the remaining grated Parmesan.

vegetables

I love vegetables. I always have. I grew up in rural Lincolnshire where locally grown produce could be bought from small shops dotted along the roadside. Potatoes came by the sack, carrots, peas and courgettes were carefully selected and popped into brown paper bags. Summer fruits would be picked from plants on the local farms. To this day, Lincolnshire grows some of the best vegetables in the UK. Over recent years I have become an enthusiastic home-grower of vegetables in my garden in East London, with as many failures as successes, and forever trying to keep the snails at bay. Sicily, however, is truly something else.

Sicilian produce is staggering and awe inspiring. It is an island that is, to all intents and purposes, self-sufficient, fuelled by the strong Sicilian sun and its fertile volcanic soil which, when combined with the brilliance of the Arab-conceived irrigation systems, means that crops of huge variety and great flavour are grown the island over. Through the seasons Sicily's market stalls heave with ever-changing local produce, delivering an enviable diet of great and wondrous variety.

I remember my first visit to the island, walking the streets of Palermo and Catania, and coming across lines of little battered old trucks parked up around the town squares, full to the brim with dazzling tomatoes, courgettes, aubergines, squashes, apricots and peaches, all brighter and bigger than I'd ever seen before.

These well-weathered old trucks were manned by well-weathered old men proudly displaying and selling produce from their farms and small holdings. Excited queues gathered by the vans with women buying daily vegetables, checking and prodding and inspecting the produce with instinctive and finely honed antennae for seeking out the very best – tomatoes from one van, bunches of fresh herbs from another and then fruits from the last van on the left of the square by the church. Then the larger, smarter vans

would pull up and fill up their boxes ready to be taken to the city markets to sell on to yet more Sicilian households, cafés and restaurants. And then, finally, you'd see local chefs arriving, filling bags to the brim ready for their daily menus and their eager customers.

Summer months in Sicily see emerald green peas and beans, so fresh and tender they are often eaten raw or dressed simply with a squeeze of lemon and a pinch of salt.

Tomatoes thrive in the Sicilian climate, often enjoyed in a simple salad with sea salt, tossed through some pasta or roasted and stuffed with breadcrumbs and anchovies. I would visit Sicily just for its tomatoes.

Huge juicy watermelons are found in abundance, to eat just as they are or to turn into a jelly or *granita* or eat alongside a salty cheese. Meanwhile stone fruits such as peaches and apricots taste as if they have been ever so slowly cooked in the sun so as to intensify their juices and turn them almost to sweet-sour caramel.

Perhaps the most iconic of Sicilian vegetables is the shiny purple aubergine, a glorious gift from the Moorish occupation and now a staple of the island's diet. *Caponata*, *involtini*, *pasta alla Norma* or simply fried and served with honey – the aubergine is inextricably linked to and synonymous with Sicily's wonderfully versatile culinary repertoire.

Then there are the Bronte pistachios. Green gold in colour, grown around Mount Etna, these pistachios have a DOP (*Denominazione di Origine Protetta* or Protected Designation of Origin) status and are considered the best in the world. When available I make the most of them, using them for ice creams, salads, dressings, picadas and dukkahs.

Courgettes are a favourite of mine and the seasonal Sicilian varieties are quite different from the sometimes rather watery ones grown in the UK. Dense fleshed and sweet, they are ideal for roasting and frying. And their flowers, when stuffed with cheese and fried (see page 64), are incredible.

Walk through any of Sicily's markets and one of the biggest displays will be of spikey artichokes, piled high and prepared for you to take away. I like to cook them as they do in the markets, over a smoky barbecue until tender, served with sea salt and lemon.

With the winter come citrus in all their varieties – lemons, oranges, blood oranges, clementines, satsumas, the aromatic scented bergamot and the gigantic cedro, a type of lemon like you've never seen, more pith than fruit but you can eat the whole thing. January and February are the prime harvesting months which seems at odds with the fresh, vital vibrancy of the fruits. I make dressings, sorbets and *granite*, put them in salads with burrata and bitter chicories, bake into custards for tarts or grill to caramelise the juices to serve with fish and meat.

The winter also brings bitter vegetables and bright leaves – green chard and kale, turnip tops and cavolo nero. I like to do as they do in Sicily and blanche them before gently tossing with olive oil and chilli, perhaps some lemon, to eat as is or mixed through pasta. Chicories, too, are prime in the winter and I like adding them to salads with a sweet vinegar dressing, a few segments of blood orange and some crunchy almonds.

The recipes in this chapter are all vegetable-focused; some happen to be vegan, some vegetarian and some have an element of meat or of fish – but the stars of the show are the vegetables! And whilst I've waxed lyrical about Sicilian produce, it is entirely possible to get the good stuff here, whether imported or grown. Just buy the best you can.

Burrata on Bruschetta
with stewed courgettes and fennel with marjoram

I love fresh Italian cheeses such as ricotta, mozzarella and stracciatella, but burrata sits top of the list. Burrata is essentially mozzarella, which is made from cow or buffalo milk, on the outside, filled with extra creamy stracciatella on the inside; when you cut it open, it oozes out in the most deliciously enticing way. I sometimes use it for cooking where it works brilliantly in my Aubergine Parmigiana (see page 149). But the super fresh cheese – burrata should ideally be eaten within 24 hours of being made – is best eaten very simply with some bruschetta and vegetables.

The stewed courgettes and fennel can be made in a larger quantity and then stored in the fridge to be served with grilled meats and fish.

Serves 4

4 x 120g pieces of very fresh burrata
4 slices of sourdough bread

For the stewed vegetables
extra virgin olive oil for cooking
   and drizzling
1 garlic clove, finely chopped
1 banana shallot, sliced
1 bay leaf

a sprig of rosemary
1 fennel bulb, cored and finely sliced
500g courgettes, trimmed and
   finely sliced
1 tablespoon red wine vinegar
1 teaspoon demerara sugar
marjoram leaves
sea salt and freshly ground
   black pepper

First make the stewed vegetables. Heat a heavy-based saucepan over a low heat and add a lug of extra virgin olive oil followed by the garlic, shallot, bay leaf and rosemary. Cook gently until very soft but without colour. Now add the sliced fennel and cook for 5 minutes or until tender. Add the courgettes and sprinkle in the vinegar, sugar and some seasoning. Stir, then simmer everything together for 20 minutes or so until tender. Cool before transferring to a bowl and chill for at least 2 hours (or overnight).

Remove the burrata and stewed vegetables from the fridge.

Heat a ridged cast-iron grill pan. Rub the sourdough slices with extra virgin olive oil and season. Grill to colour both sides. Place these bruschetta on plates.

Spoon the courgette and fennel stew on to the bruschetta and top with the burrata. Season the burrata and drizzle over some extra virgin olive oil, then sprinkle with marjoram leaves.

Sweet and Sour Peppers

Preservation is a popular technique in Sicily to ensure that there are good things to eat in frugal times or out of season.

Though I can buy fresh peppers in my local supermarket all the year round, I will always have a jar of these delicious sweet and sour preserved peppers in my fridge. I make them in a large batch and then eke them out over a few weeks – they actually get even better over time. I use them in many ways; everything from a simple topping on warm flatbreads as a snack or to accompanying grilled chicken or fish. I even sometimes stir some into a ragù towards then end of cooking to add depth and a boost of flavour.

Serves 6–8

10 pointy peppers
olive oil for cooking
100ml sweet white wine vinegar
   (such as moscatel)
100ml water
40g golden caster sugar
4 bay leaves

10 sprigs of thyme
2 garlic cloves, finely sliced
10 black peppercorns
a good pinch of saffron threads
180ml quality Sicilian extra virgin
   olive oil
sea salt

Preheat the oven to 210°C/190°C fan/Gas Mark 6–7.

Place the whole peppers in a roasting tin, drizzle with olive oil and roast, turning once or twice, for 25–30 minutes or until softened and starting to blacken. Remove from the oven, cover the tray with foil and leave for 20 minutes to cool.

Meanwhile, place the rest of the ingredients in a saucepan. Set over a medium heat and bring to the boil, then simmer for 10 minutes. Reserve this marinade.

When the peppers have cooled, carefully peel off the skin, then slit the peppers down the middle and remove the seeds. You may need to rinse quickly with cold water to ensure all seeds are removed. I like to keep the pepper tops attached to give a rustic, natural appearance.

Place the peppers in a bowl and pour over the marinade. Cover and leave in the fridge for 24 hours. They will be delicious after this time but can be kept for at least 3 weeks and get better with time.

To serve, take what you need with some of the marinade and serve at room temperature as antipasti or a side dish.

Fritella

Not to be confused with *frittella*, the Sicilian fried delights, this dish is its antithesis. It is the epitome of spring and typically Sicilian in preparation, featuring three ingredients at their seasonal prime – baby artichokes, peas and broad beans. The dish lives and dies by these three vegetables, oh, and the extra virgin olive oil it's bathed in! Tinned, dried or from a jar doesn't really work here, whether from a flavour or a visual perspective. Bright and sparkling, this is spring on a plate.

Serves 4

4 violet artichokes
lemon juice
300g fresh peas
600g fresh young broad beans
1 large banana shallot, finely sliced

100ml extra virgin olive oil
1 tablespoon white wine vinegar
a handful of mint leaves
sea salt and freshly ground
    black pepper

Prepare the artichokes by taking off any hard outer leaves or spiky parts, then cut each artichoke into quarters lengthways. As they are prepared drop them into water mixed with lemon juice to prevent them from discolouring. Pod the peas and the beans.

In a medium sauté pan over a low heat sweat the sliced shallot in some of the extra virgin olive oil until soft. Drain the artichokes and add to the pan along with the peas, beans and 100ml of water. Season and cover with a lid. Cook on a low heat for about 25 minutes, stirring every 5 minutes and ensuring there is always some liquid in the pan (if necessary, add more water).

Add the vinegar to the mint and stir well, then add to the fritella and cook for another couple of minutes. By the end of cooking the liquid should have almost disappeared though the fritella should not be dry.

Add the rest of the olive oil, stir and leave to sit for 10 minutes before serving. Delicious with some shaved pecorino or Parmesan and served with Focaccia (see page 22).

Aeolian-style Summer Salad

This dish is all about the tomatoes. It's hard to perfectly replicate a delicious, fresh salad from Sicily's Aeolian islands when in the UK, yet we produce many delicious varieties of tomatoes that will stand up well in comparison. I'd use a plum vine or a Bull's Heart tomato – ensure they are ripe, but not over ripe.

I like to use a sweet-sour grape must (*saba*) for the dressing, which is smoother and fruitier than a vinegar, but an aged balsamic will also do nicely.

Serves 4

10 medium-sized, medium-ripe, sweet red tomatoes (vine-ripened are best), sliced into rounds
2 tablespoons plump capers
2 handfuls of pitted green olives
2 tropea onions or small red onions, finely sliced
6 anchovies in oil, chopped
1 tablespoon oregano leaves
10 basil leaves, torn

For the vinaigrette
2 tablespoons saba (grape must) or balsamic vinegar
4 tablespoons extra virgin olive oil
sea salt and freshly ground black pepper

Whisk together the grape must and extra virgin olive oil. Season to taste.

To assemble the salad, carefully arrange the tomato slices on a serving plate and sprinkle over the capers, olives, onions, anchovies and herbs. Season well, then drizzle over the vinaigrette.

Leave the salad for 5 minutes, so all the flavours come together, before serving.

Chilled Green Beans
with toasted almonds, shallots, raisins and orange

Why eat a steaming plate of hot vegetables in the sweltering heat of a Sicilian summer when you have delicious vegetables to hand that taste great when served cold?

This lovely salad is my homage to one I enjoyed at a little restaurant on Panera, one of the magical Aeolian islands off the Sicilian coast. The vibrancy and simplicity of the salad stayed long in the memory and I created my own version once I was back home.

The sweet oranges and raisins and the crunchy almonds and shallots balance the freshly blanched chilled green beans. Sun-drenched and delicious.

Serves 4

340g fresh, crisp green beans, trimmed
a handful of fresh nibbed almonds
2 small, sweet oranges, peeled of skin
   and pith
50ml red wine vinegar
75ml extra virgin olive oil
½ teaspoon caster sugar

1 tablespoon raisins, soaked in warm
   water to plump
1 banana shallot, very finely sliced
   crossways
sea salt and freshly ground
   black pepper

Cook the green beans in plenty of boiling salted water until just tender. Drain immediately in a colander and refresh under running cold water with a few ice cubes added. This part of the process is very important – you want to lock in the vibrant green of the beans and arrest the cooking process. Drain the beans again and transfer to a kitchen towel-lined, then plate in the fridge.

Place a sauté pan over a medium heat and add the almonds. Toast them until they are an even golden brown, tossing them every few seconds to prevent burning. Remove from the pan and cool, then roughly chop.

Segment the oranges with a sharp knife, working over a bowl to capture any juice.

Whisk together the vinegar, reserved orange juice, olive oil and sugar and season well.

To serve, place the beans in a salad bowl. Spoon over the vinaigrette, season and mix well. Stir in the raisins and shallot. Sprinkle over the chopped almonds and spoon around the orange segments. Serve.

Watermelon, Chicory and Salty Pecorino Salad

Watermelons are the perfect summer food: fresh, juicy, vibrant and cooling. Nature's antidote to a swelteringly hot day. Here I've used it as the base of a simple salad of bitter chicory, crunchy green pistachio and salty hard pecorino cheese. Add a simple dressing and a few herbs and you have an incredible summer lunch or accompaniment to grilled fish or meat.

Serves 4–6

1 small, heavy watermelon (choose one with unblemished, smooth, shiny skin)
2 small heads red chicory, stalks trimmed and leaves separated
50ml sweet white wine vinegar (e.g. moscatel or white balsamic)
65g green Iranian pistachios

150g aged pecorino cheese such as Sardo (or a good aged Parmesan), cut into irregular shards
70ml groundnut oil
a handful of wild fennel fronds, fennel herb or dill
sea salt and freshly ground black pepper

Cut the melon in half through the width and reserve half for another use.

Peel the skin and white pith from the watermelon half, then dice the flesh into 2cm pieces. Place in a bowl along with the chicory leaves. Season and mix in the vinegar. Reserve.

Place a sauté pan over a medium heat and add the pistachios to toast for a few minutes, tossing them, until they are fragrant and have started to release their oil. Season liberally with salt and mix with the watermelon. Now fold in the pecorino and add the groundnut oil and fennel fronds. Briefly mix again, then arrange on a platter or plates so you can see all the elements. Serve.

Chilled Fennel and Broad Bean Soup

My old friend and fellow chef Antonio moved to the island of Pantellaria a few years ago and I try to make time to visit him at least twice during the summer months. Pantellaria is less crazy than the rest of Sicily and affords a peaceful respite and helps me recharge my culinary batteries. Situated just off Sicily's south-west coast and a stone's throw from Tunisia, the island retains a unique dialect incorporating a sort of slang Arabic mixed with Italian. The otherworldly landscape is stunning, at once both beautiful and strange, with its volcanic, alien-like *terroir* and craters, natural bubbling springs and black volcanic, tiered cliffs.

Antonio is not only a very chilled character to be around but also a talented cook and he makes a soup very similar to this one to help combat the sweltering August island heat. It is delicious and perfect to be enjoyed in the midday shade.

Serves 4

extra virgin olive oil for cooking
1 very fresh fennel bulb, finely sliced
25g blanched almonds
1 litre chicken or vegetable stock
  (home-made is best)
20g crème fraîche

lemon juice
1 teaspoon fennel seeds
100g podded young broad beans
a handful of wild fennel fronds or dill
sea salt and freshly ground
  black pepper

Heat a medium saucepan over a medium heat and add a lug of olive oil. Add the fennel and cook briskly, without colouring, until softened. Now add the almonds and stock and bring to the boil, then simmer for 5 minutes or so until the fennel is fully cooked through and the almonds have softened. Season and add the crème fraîche. Transfer to a blender and blitz for 5 minutes or until smooth.

Season to taste and add some lemon juice. Pour into a container and chill.

Heat a little oil in a small saucepan over a medium heat and lightly fry the fennel seeds until they become fragrant. Transfer to a pestle and mortar and crush lightly. Mix the fennel seeds with the broad beans and fennel fronds or dill.

Pour the soup into chilled bowls, spoon in some of the bean and fennel seed mix, and serve. Ideal on a sweltering hot day.

Sicilian Lentil and Ditalina Soup

Each region in Italy has its version of *pasta e lenticchie*. On the face of it 'pasta mixed into lentil soup' may sound a little dreary and beige, however with a little care the reality is one of a robustly flavoured, heart-warming soup. A bowlful will set you in good stead for the day. My Sicilian version is infused with a little chilli kick and some fragrant lemon leaves which, along with the heady oregano, adds a sunny Mediterranean undertone.

Serves 4

extra virgin olive oil
75g guanciale or pancetta, finely chopped (optional)
1 medium-sized onion, finely chopped
2 garlic cloves, crushed and finely chopped
1 carrot, finely chopped
1 celery stick, finely chopped
1 small, fresh red chilli, finely chopped
4 plum tomatoes (either fresh or canned), roughly chopped
300g small brown or grey lentils, rinsed

4 unsprayed lemon leaves
1–2 sprigs of flat-leaf parsley, roughly chopped
350g short tubular pasta such as ditalina
a handful of grated pecorino cheese
1 tablespoon roughly chopped oregano leaves
sea salt and freshly ground black pepper

In a medium saucepan or deep sauté pan, warm the olive oil over a medium heat, then add the guanciale (if using), the onion, garlic, carrot, celery, chilli and a pinch of salt. Sauté the ingredients, stirring and turning them regularly, until they are very soft and golden brown, which should take about 15 minutes.

Add the tomatoes to the pan and stir them in, then cook for another few minutes. Add the lentils, turning them 2 or 3 times to coat them well with the vegetable mixture. Stir in the lemon leaves and parsley. Add enough water to cover the lentils plus 2–3cm extra. Bring the contents of the pan to the boil, then reduce the heat so the lentils and vegetables are simmering gently. Cook, stirring every now and then, for about 30 minutes or until the lentils are tender. Make sure the water level is always about 2cm above the lentils, so replenish as needed.

Season, then taste and add more seasoning if necessary. Add the pasta and raise the heat so the lentil and pasta mixture is boiling gently. Keep stirring attentively as the pasta will tend to stick to the bottom of the pan; add more water if necessary. Once the pasta is cooked (tender but still with a slight bite) remove from the heat and let the pan sit for 5 minutes.

Serve with a little extra virgin olive oil poured on top along with some grated pecorino and a liberal sprinkling of fresh oregano.

Braised Chickpeas and Borlotti Beans
with kale 'pesto'

This braise is in between a hearty soup and a light stew and perfect for the winter months. It's just the kind of meal you want to keep the cold out, with the cumin seeds adding their warming, exotic undertones, infusing throughout the dish.

The kale 'pesto' is a nice fresh addition stirred in just before serving, adding more body to the soup. I use the pesto for lots of things including tossing through hot oily pasta and spooning over grilled fish.

Serves 4–6

400g canned chickpeas, drained and rinsed
400g canned borlotti beans, drained and rinsed
2 bay leaves
1 garlic clove (unpeeled)
1 white onion, finely chopped
1 teaspoon cumin seeds
olive oil for cooking
500g ripe tomatoes, peeled and roughly chopped

For the kale 'pesto'
a handful of flat-leaf parsley
a large handful of chopped seasonal kale (such as cavolo nero)
50g blanched almonds
a squeeze of lemon juice
50ml extra virgin olive oil
1 tablespoon pine nuts
2 garlic cloves, peeled
sea salt and freshly ground black pepper

Put the chickpeas and borlotti beans in a medium flameproof casserole along with the bay leaves and garlic clove. Cover with water, set over a medium heat and bring to the boil, then simmer for 40 minutes or until the chickpeas and beans are very soft. Remove from the heat and leave to cool in the liquor.

In another saucepan, sweat the onion and cumin seeds in olive oil for a few minutes to soften the onion and release the aroma from the spice. Now add the tomatoes and cook for 30 minutes or so, crushing the tomatoes with a ladle as you go, until reduced to a sauce consistency.

Add a ladleful of the chickpea liquor to the tomato sauce, then spoon in the chickpeas and beans (reserve the remaining chickpea liquor). Simmer for a few minutes and season well.

To make the pesto, put everything in a blender and blitz to a rustic purée.

Spoon the pesto into the braised borlotti beans and chickpeas. If needed, add more of the remaining chickpea liquor to loosen, then serve. This is delicious with my home-made Mafalda bread on page 20 or a chewy sourdough.

Caponata

Sicilian *caponata* traces its origins back to the Catalan region of Spain. The Catalan word *caponada* is a similar type of vegetable preparation, translating as 'tied together with vines' referring to the tomato base.

Originally created to be eaten by sailors on long sea voyages, the addition of a heavy dose of vinegar acted as a highly effective and much needed preservative.

Caponata today is a refined dish with many versions appearing throughout Sicily. I love its mouth puckering sweet-sour piquancy and I have been working on perfecting this specific recipe for years. The cocoa powder adds a bitterness that seems to pull everything together. I make a big batch and store it in a Kilner jar in the fridge – it only gets better with time. Delicious served with warm bread as a snack.

Serves 8

1 large aubergine (about 500g), cut into 2cm dice
1 large courgette, cut into 2cm dice
vegetable or sunflower oil for frying
3 tablespoons olive oil
1 large red onion, sliced
2 celery sticks, cut into 2cm dice
1½ teaspoons dried chilli flakes (optional)
150g ripe tomatoes, diced

40g capers
40g pitted green olives, quartered
40g sultanas or raisins
1 tablespoon sugar
150ml tomato passata
100ml red wine vinegar
1 tablespoon grated dark chocolate
40g toasted almonds or pine nuts
a small bunch of mint, leaves picked
sea salt

Lightly salt the diced aubergine and courgette and put them in a colander set in the sink, trying to keep them in 2 distinct layers. Leave to drain for at least 30 minutes, then pat dry.

Heat a wide, deep pan one-third full of vegetable oil until it reaches 190°C (a breadcrumb dropped into the oil will brown immediately). Fry the aubergine and courgette in batches (being careful not to overcrowd the pan) until golden, allowing the oil to come back up to temperature between frying the batches. Drain on kitchen paper.

Heat the olive oil in a large, wide pan (for which you have a lid) over a medium-low heat. Add the onion and celery with a pinch of salt and fry until soft and beginning to colour, then stir in the chilli flakes, if using, and fry for a further minute. Add the diced tomatoes and fry for another couple of minutes.

Stir in the capers, olives, sultanas or raisins, sugar, passata, vinegar and chocolate and bring to the boil, then add the fried aubergines and courgettes and season. Turn the heat right down, cover and simmer gently for 1 hour, checking towards the end of cooking and taking the pan off the heat if the caponata seems to be drying out.

Remove from the heat and allow to cool to room temperature, then check the seasoning. Meanwhile, toast the almonds in a dry frying pan. Add them, along with the roughly torn mint, just before serving.

Grilled Garden Onions
wrapped in guanciale

I first tried this dish at the Giarratana annual onion festival, a wonderful celebration of this prized onion in all its glory. The fatty *guanciale* (cured pigs' cheek) slowly melts over the onion adding a salty, porky flavour and keeps the onions moist, basting them with its fat.

In the UK I use the large, bulbous garden onions with long green stems and if I can't get *guanciale* then I'll use a really good pancetta. Perfect for a barbecue but also great when cooked on a griddle.

Serves 4

2 bunches of large, bulbous garden/
   salad onions, green stalks intact
extra virgin olive oil for cooking
10–12 long, thin slices of guanciale or
   pancetta (1 slice for each onion)

lemon juice
pine nut and saffron sauce
   (see page 286) to serve
sea salt and freshly ground
   black pepper

Prepare a barbecue or heat a ridged cast-iron grill pan to medium heat. Brush the onions with a little olive oil and season them well, then place on the grill. Cook them, turning as you go, to char the stalks and to start to soften the onion heads. After 3–4 minutes (or when the onions are half cooked) remove them and cool slightly.

Wrap each onion in a slice of guanciale to cover the length. If using a barbecue, finish cooking the onions to the side of the fire in a cooler spot; on a grill pan, lower the heat. The onions are ready when the bulb is nice and tender and the guanciale has turned golden brown.

Squeeze over some lemon juice and serve with the pine nut and saffron sauce.

Swiss Chard Gratin
with ricotta, mascarpone and pine nuts

I love these sturdy winter greens. There's something about eating them that makes you feel well nourished.

I normally cook the Swiss chard very simply – sliced and then cooked in olive oil with chilli, garlic, lemon and a splash of water to finish. However, for a special occasion, I like to bake them into gratin with creamy ricotta, spiked with lemon and black pepper and finished with a crunchy crust of breadcrumbs and pine nuts.

I'd happily eat this as the star of the show, with perhaps a green salad to accompany, but you could also serve it as part of a Sicilian-inspired feast – both my Veal Braciolie on page 220 or Whole Roast Chicken on page 200 would pair very well.

Serves 6

olive oil for cooking
750g swiss chard, leaves and
   stalks separated
150ml mascarpone
150g sheep's ricotta

zest and juice of ½ unwaxed lemon
100g dried coarse breadcrumbs
50g pine nuts
sea salt and freshly ground
   black pepper

Heat a large sauté pan over a low heat and add a lug of oil. Slice the chard stalks into strips, then throw them into the pan and season well. Cook for 2–3 minutes to soften. Add the chard leaves and cook these for a minute or so to wilt. Remove from the heat.

Preheat the oven to 200°C/180°C fan/Gas Mark 6.

Whisk together the mascarpone, ricotta, and lemon zest and juice. Season with salt and plenty of pepper. Add the chard and its juices to the mascarpone-ricotta mix and stir through. Transfer to an ovenproof dish and drizzle over a little olive oil. Place in the oven and bake for 12 minutes or until the gratin is hot and has started to bubble. Remove from the oven to rest.

Mix together the breadcrumbs, pine nuts and some olive oil. Sprinkle the crumbs evenly over the top of the gratin. Place back in the oven to bake for 10–12 minutes or until the top is golden brown and crunchy and the gratin is bubbling away. Serve immediately at the table.

Smokey Artichokes
with lemon, parsley and garlic

If there's one thing I'll be getting on my barbecue over the summer months, it is these Sicilian market staples. Artichokes are abundant in Sicily during the summer and you'll find markets and street corners filled with smoke as vendors throw oil and salt-laden spikey chokes onto the flames. The leaves of the artichoke insulate and protect the delicate choke within whilst taking on the smokiness of the barbecue. You can use baby artichokes or the larger ones, just alter the time accordingly.

Best eaten the Sicilian way – with your hands, charred and glistening.

Serves 6

6 medium-sized artichokes,
   or 12 baby artichokes
3 tablespoons finely chopped
   flat-leaf parsley
200ml olive oil

2 garlic cloves, finely chopped
juice of 1 lemon
sea salt and freshly ground
   black pepper

Prepare a medium-hot charcoal fire or heat a ridged cast-iron grill pan.

Trim off the top end and stem of each medium-sized artichoke level with the base. If using baby artichokes, you can grill them with leaves and stem attached.

Whisk together 2 tablespoons of the parsley, the olive oil and garlic and season. Spread the leaves of the artichokes apart with your fingers, or by banging the bottom on a hard surface, and slowly pour the dressing over the top, making sure it drips into all the spaces between the leaves. Alternatively, you can split the artichokes in half lengthways and coat the cut sides with the dressing.

Place the artichokes on the barbecue grill or in the embers of the coals, or on the grill pan, cut sides up if halved. If cooking in the embers, turn while cooking until the outside leaves are black; if cooking on the barbecue grill or pan, cook until the bottoms of the artichokes are easily pierced with a long wooden skewer. This will take about 45 minutes for whole medium-sized artichokes, 25 minutes for halved or baby artichokes.

Remove the artichokes to a platter, drizzle with the lemon juice mixed with the remaining parsley and serve. Eat the artichokes with your hands!

Aubergine Parmigiana

Contrary to popular opinion, this delightful and indulgent slab of Mediterranean comfort food hails from the south. Whilst its eponymous namesake, Parmesan or Parmigiana, originates from the north of Italy, the other key ingredients, aubergines, tomatoes and mozzarella (or burrata in this case, as I find it makes its own creamy sauce) are from the south, and into Sicily.

Wherever it comes from, it's a classic and known worldwide. At Norma I elevate it to include a rich Parmesan cream (similar to the sauce for the crispy potatoes on page 52, if you want to try) that was poured over at the end, for extra indulgence, and crispy basil leaves strewn over at the end. It's one of the most popular of our dishes, and probably the most instagrammed dish on the menu.

Serves 6–7

1.2kg or 2 litres quality canned chopped tomatoes
150g fresh cherry tomatoes, cut in half
8 aubergines, ends trimmed
extra virgin olive oil
250g dried breadcrumbs

a handful of basil, leaves picked
4 x 120g burrata, drained
250g Parmesan cheese, grated
sea salt and freshly ground black pepper

Put the canned and fresh tomatoes into a saucepan and simmer over a medium heat to slowly reduce by half. Reserve.

Cut the aubergines lengthways into slices about 2cm thick.

Heat a large, heavy-based frying pan over a medium heat. Pour in some olive oil and, when hot, gently fry the aubergines slices, in batches, until tender and golden brown on both sides. You will need to add extra oil as you go as the aubergines soak it up quite quickly. When the slices are fried, season well and drain on kitchen paper.

Preheat the oven to 200°C/180°C fan/Gas Mark 6.

Rub the inside of an ovenproof dish (I use a terracotta or a metal dish for a rustic look) with olive oil. Make a layer of aubergine slices on the bottom, then sprinkle with breadcrumbs and a few basil leaves followed by a ladleful of tomato sauce, a burrata ripped into pieces and a handful of Parmesan. Ensure everything is evenly spread, then continue layering this way, finishing with a layer of aubergine. Reserve some breadcrumbs, Parmesan and basil.

Bake for 40 minutes or until the parmigiana is bubbling away and the aubergines on top have begun to crisp.

Remove from the oven to rest for 20 minutes, then sprinkle with the reserved breadcrumbs and Parmesan, and finish under a hot grill for 5 minutes. Scatter the remaining basil leaves on top before serving.

Baked Squash
with ricotta, sage, chilli and lemon

As autumn comes to the island, a whole array of colourful squash begins to appear. Baking them this way intensifies their natural sweetness making a perfect vessel for a rich, warming filling.

Different squashes have different types of flesh. You should be on the lookout for those with a heavier, denser flesh that will roast well. A carnival or an onion squash would be perfect.

Serves 4

4 equal-sized round squashes, such as
   onion squash, about 500–600g each
100ml crème fraîche
100g ricotta cheese
1 fresh red chilli, deseeded and
   finely sliced
½ teaspoon ground cinnamon

zest and juice of ½ unwaxed lemon
olive oil for drizzling
75g pecorino or Parmesan cheese,
   finely grated
12 sage leaves
sea salt and freshly ground
   black pepper

Preheat the oven to 200°C/180°C fan/Gas Mark 6.

Cut the top (stalk end) off each squash, then scoop out the seeds and fibres plus a little of the flesh to enlarge the cavity (discard this flesh). Place the squashes cut side up in a roasting tray. It's important they stand up straight. If they don't, sit them in a 'nest' of baking foil to prop them up. Also put the cut lids in the tray.

Mix the crème fraîche with the ricotta, chilli, cinnamon, lemon zest and juice, and seasoning. Fill the cavities in the squash with the ricotta mix, then drizzle oil over the tops and lids and season again.

Lay a sheet of foil over the squashes and crimp it around the tray. Bake for about 50 minutes to 1 hour or until the squashes are tender – a knife inserted into the skin should glide through.

Remove the foil. Sprinkle the grated pecorino or Parmesan over the squashes and top them with the sage leaves. Turn the oven up to 240°C/220°C fan/Gas Mark 9.

Place the squashes back in the oven to bake for 15–20 minutes or until the cheese on top has browned.

Serve immediately with crusty bread to dip into the molten ricotta filling.

Stuffed and Baked Tomatoes
with fried breadcrumbs, anchovies and sheep's cheese

There's something exotic and 1980s about stuffing fruits and vegetables but Sicilians have been using this method for many hundreds of years.

Be sure to use less than fully ripe tomatoes so they cook nicely and securely around the stuffing without collapsing.

Serves 4

4 large flavoursome tomatoes (such as Marmande or Bull's Heart)
50g crème fraîche
125g medium-soft sheep's cheese or goat's cheese (a feta is very good)
1 small, fresh red chilli, deseeded and finely chopped
a handful of marjoram leaves

2 salted anchovies, finely chopped
juice of ½ lemon
olive oil
1 slice of sourdough bread, crusts removed and roughly chopped to coarse breadcrumbs
sea salt and freshly ground black pepper

Slice the top from each tomato about 1cm down (reserve these lids) and take a very thin slice from the base so the tomato will stand straight. Carefully scoop out the seeds and pulp using a spoon and a sharp paring knife (keep the seeds and pulp for use in a tomato sauce).

Preheat the oven to 200°C/180°C fan/Gas Mark 6.

In a bowl whisk together the crème fraîche, cheese, chilli, half the marjoram, the anchovies and lemon juice. Season well.

Stuff the tomatoes with the cheese mix right up to the top. Place the tomatoes on a baking tray, drizzle with oil and season. Place in the oven and bake for 15 minutes or until the tomatoes have started to soften and the skin started to blister. The filling should have started to bubble. Now add the reserved tomato lids to the tray and bake for a further 5 minutes. The tomatoes should be well cooked with a molten filling.

While the tomatoes are cooking, fry the breadcrumbs in hot olive oil until golden brown and nicely crisp.

Remove the tomatoes from the oven and rest for 2 minutes before sprinkling over the breadcrumbs and the remaining marjoram. Top with the lids. Serve as part of a selection of antipasti. I like to eat this with my Sicilian Fritella on page 126.

Fried Spinach, Courgette and Lemon Cakes

These unusual and delicious fritters are popular on the island in the springtime when there's often a glut of courgettes and spinach. The ricotta is my addition – I think it adds a lovely creamy richness. The bulgur wheat not only gives substance to the cakes but also has the most wonderful, nutty flavour.

Bulgur wheat is perhaps not immediately associated with the island, but there's a particular Sicilian variety, gezzina, that is very popular. Sicily has been a grain-rich land since very early Neolithic times and lately there's been a resurgence of interest in the old varieties such as timilia and maiorca.

Serves 4

200g bulgur wheat, rinsed and soaked in cold water for 2 hours
olive oil for cooking
2 onions, finely chopped
2 garlic cloves, finely chopped
3 courgettes
200g baby spinach, finely sliced
2 free-range eggs
75g drained ricotta

1 unwaxed lemon
½ bunch of mint, leaves picked and finely chopped
1 teaspoon Sicilian-style roasted chilli sauce (see page 280) or 1 fresh red chilli, finely chopped and mixed with 1 teaspoon extra virgin olive oil
sea salt and freshly ground black pepper

Cook the bulgur wheat according to the packet instructions (about 12 minutes from soaked). Drain and leave to steam dry.

Heat a medium sauté pan over a medium heat and add a lug of olive oil. Add the onions and garlic and cook for about 10 minutes or until softened but without colour.

Coarsely grate the courgettes into the pan, then add the spinach. Cook for a further 1–2 minutes or until the spinach has wilted and the courgettes have softened slightly. Spoon the mixture into a bowl along with the bulgur wheat and leave to cool completely.

Preheat the oven to 220°C/200°C fan/Gas Mark 7.

Crack the eggs into the bowl and stir in with the ricotta. Finely grate the lemon zest into the mixture and squeeze in half the juice. Add most of the mint and the chilli sauce. Give everything a good stir, then season.

With wet hands, divide the mixture into 12. Shape into balls, then flatten into cakes about 2.5cm thick. Heat a large sauté pan over a medium heat, add a good amount of olive oil and, when hot, add the cakes. Fry them until golden brown on both sides (you may need to do this in 2 batches). Transfer to an oven tray and place in the oven. Cook for 15 minutes or until piping hot and fully cooked through.

Scatter the remaining mint leaves and more sea salt over the cakes and serve as antipasti, on their own or with my salmoriglio on page 281.

fish

The Sicilians' determined and staunch demand for using only the freshest and best produce available is a constant source of wonder to me. And fish is no exception.

Situated in the heart of the Mediterranean Sicily is blessed with an abundance of fish and shellfish. An outside observer might reasonably imagine that fish and seafood would be integral to the life of the whole island and to the Sicilian diet in general. And yet, by the very nature of the way that most Sicilians live their lives, always eating locally and seasonally, seafood is eaten mainly along the coast. And so it is that a brief 20km drive inland is considered by most Sicilians to be far too long a journey to keep the just-caught fish suitably fresh to put on the table.

The Sicilians cook their fish simply, often stuffed with or coated in *pan grattato* (breadcrumbs) and then fried. You'll find a version of *fritto misto* in every bar and restaurant on the coast – one of my favourite snacks, especially if it includes sardines and squid, to be washed down with an icy Messina beer.

Sicilians have a love affair with fire and understand the profound benefits of cooking seafood over flames; the smoky wood and charcoal transforming the fish to juicy and charred perfection. The heady aromas of grilling seafood never fail to evoke in me the nostalgic memories of wonderful Sicilian holidays and delicious long lunches on the harbour side.

Sicilians love raw fish, and it is the their love of *crudo* fish dishes in particular that sets them up to compete against the raw fish wonders of Japanese *sashimi* and *Peruvian* ceviche.

As with most Sicilian cooking, *crudo* preparation is simple and the ingredients few. A good *crudo* needs nothing more than citrus to cure, olive oil to enrich and herbs to flavour. From the sea to the table in a few minutes – glorious in its purity and perfection.

Tuna is a particular passion of the Sicilian table, with a whole industry built around its supply and demand. The tuna fisheries with their traps and nets are now mostly disused, but a few remain open to visit.

In Sicily all and every part of the tuna is enjoyed and celebrated. Nose to tail eating at its finest.

A trip to a fish market when visiting Sicily is a must. Sicilian fish markets are a vibrant, bustling, rowdy revelation. With the island surrounded by seas – the Mediterranean lapping along the west and south coasts, the Ionian Sea lying to the east and the Tyrrhenian Sea rolling onto the north – sourcing freshly caught fish is easy and buying a dazzling specimen at a local market should be at the top of any visitor's list.

Fish of all types and denominations are displayed – squid, octopus, sea urchins, cuttlefish and all imaginable varieties of shellfish present themselves to eager purchasers. The star of the show is the regal tuna, reigning magnificent in appearance and dramatic in its display. Swordfish too can be seen in all their splendour, but less so now as their stocks are protected and supplies dwindle.

TAnd behind the glitter and the glamour of the showstopping species often hide two Sicilian specialities not to be missed – *bottarga* and *mosciame*.

Bottarga is the salted, dried and hard-pressed roe of the female tuna. Grated like Parmesan, it is used to flavour and finish dishes. It is simply wonderful. *Mosciame* is salted tuna that is sliced paper thin and can most commonly be enjoyed as part of an antipasto selection. It, too, is supberb.

Fishing is one of the major industries of the island and is in many ways the heartbeat of the Sicilian culinary culture. Small brightly painted fishing boats bob and weave gathering in their catches, occasionally rebuffing the advances of the larger fishing vessels as they make their way into the ports to offload the riches of their travails. It is a sight to relish and savour whilst sitting at seaside bars and cafés with small plates of antipasti and chilled glasses of Grillo.

Anchovies and Pickled Shallots
on pork fat toast

Pork and anchovies have always had a natural affinity. Here the salty anchovies are offset by rich, porky fried toast and sweet-sour pickled shallots making this the perfect *aperitivo* snack.

Invest in the best anchovies you can find – they are the star of the show. Ortiz and Nardin are both good brands. A delis the best starting point to find good-quality anchovies.

Serves 6

100ml cider vinegar
1 tablespoon caster sugar
1 bay leaf
1 banana shallot, sliced into thin rings
100g lard
6 thin slices of ciabatta

12 fat anchovies in oil
1 teaspoon oregano or marjoram leaves
extra virgin olive oil
sea salt and freshly ground
    black pepper

Put the vinegar, sugar and bay leaf in a saucepan and bring to the boil. Cook for 3 minutes. Cool, then add the shallot and a pinch of sea salt. Leave the shallot to pickle for at least 20 minutes.

Heat the lard in a sauté pan on a medium heat, then gently fry the bread slices until golden brown on both sides. Drain well on kitchen paper and season.

To serve top each slice of fried ciabatta with 2 anchovies, a little spoonful of the pickled shallots, some oregano or marjoram, seasoning and a little olive oil. Serve as a snack for an aperitivo.

Mackerel Crudo

with fennel, fennel pollen and preserved lemon

A super light and fresh *crudo* with the warming, curry-like notes of fennel pollen and the sweet-sour preserved lemon cutting through the mackerel's natural oiliness. This dish couldn't be simpler to prepare; however obtaining supremely fresh mackerel is paramount to its success. The fish should be nice and firm to the touch, with a vibrant pink flesh and the skin almost effervescent blue.

Serves 4 as a starter

4 medium-sized mackerel fillets, skinned and pin-boned
1 preserved lemon, halved and sliced into thin half-moons (seeds removed)
½ small fennel bulb, very finely sliced (a mandoline is good for this)

½ teaspoon fennel pollen
juice of ½ lemon
4 teaspoons extra virgin olive oil
fennel fronds to garnish
sea salt and freshly ground black pepper

Cut the mackerel into 1cm dice and place in a bowl with the preserved lemon, fennel and fennel pollen. Add the lemon juice, oil and seasoning. Mix well and leave to stand for 5 minutes before dividing among the chilled plates and sprinkling with fennel fronds.

Sea Bass Crudo
with blood orange, bottarga and marjoram

I make this *crudo* in the winter when blood oranges are in season and abundant, but actually it's good any time of year.

Bottarga is an interesting ingredient, originally hailing from Calabria but there are versions of it all around southern Italy; it's the salted and then wind-dried roe from mullets or tuna. Once dried it's wrapped in wax to preserve it. It is used as a sort of condiment, finely grated into pastas or salads, and in this recipe it is grated over the *crudo* to add a sweet-salty-umami depth. *Bottarga* is utterly delicious and available from all good Italian delis.

Serves 4

2 sea bass fillets, skinned and cut into 1cm slices
1 small blood orange (or bitter orange such as Seville), peel and pith removed
2 tablespoons sweet white wine vinegar (e.g. Chardonnay or moscatel vinegar)

2 tablespoons extra virgin olive oil
6 sprigs of marjoram, leaves picked
1 teaspoon finely grated bottarga
sea salt and freshly ground black pepper

Place the slices of fish in a bowl and season well.

Segment the blood orange with a sharp knife, working over the bowl that the fish is in – you want the juices to marinate the fish. Give the fish a stir, then leave for 10 minutes to cure.

Whisk together the vinegar and olive oil and season well.

To serve, lay the slices of fish on the plates. Drizzle a little of the vinaigrette over each plate and top with the orange segments and marjoram leaves. Finish by sprinkling over the bottarga.

Red Prawns, Orange and Thyme

The *gambero rosso*, red prawns of Sicily, are a revelation – meaty, incredibly sweet and vibrant in colour. Caught off the south-western coast of Sicily where the seafood is bountiful, they are delicious when fresh and are seldom cooked except for some light curing with salt and citrus. A fishmonger will be able to source these for you but a super fresh langoustine or a large prawn would be a decent substitute. Leave the heads on and suck out the briny, umami laden juices.

Serves 4 as a starter

100ml freshly squeezed orange juice
extra virgin olive oil
12 super-fresh, large, raw red prawns

2 teaspoons thyme leaves
sea salt

Put the orange juice in a small saucepan with a dash of extra virgin olive oil and reduce slowly by half. Cool to room temperature.

Leaving the heads on, carefully peel the shells from the prawns and discard. Gently run a very sharp paring knife down the back of each prawn tail and remove any entrails (devein). Rinse the prawns briefly in cold water. Pat them dry and place in a bowl.

Sprinkle over some sea salt, then pour over the orange dressing and leave for 5 minutes to cure lightly.

Divide the prawns among the plates. Sprinkle over the thyme and drizzle around some of the orange dressing. Serve immediately.

Clams

with lemon leaves, chilli, mint and pistachios

Sicilian east coast fishing villages serve vibrant shellfish dishes that sparkle with freshness mixed with a kiss of North Africa. This is a delicious, fragrant dish, the lemon leaves imparting a different flavour note to either lemon zest or lemon juice – a more subtle, aromatic undertone, perfect for the delicate clams. The pistachio dukkah adds nutty crunch.

Serves 4

olive oil for cooking
a handful of dried breadcrumbs
50g very green pistachios, roughly
    chopped
400g fresh palourde clams, scrubbed
    and rinsed well in cold water
200ml dry white wine

a handful of unsprayed lemon leaves
1 small, fresh red chilli, deseeded and
    finely chopped
50g unsalted butter
a handful of mint leaves, roughly
    chopped
freshly ground black pepper

Heat a good lug of olive oil in a medium sauté pan set over a medium heat. Add the breadcrumbs and fry until golden brown, then stir in the pistachios. Reserve.

Heat a large saucepan over a high heat and throw in the clams, white wine, lemon leaves and chilli. Place a lid on the pan and steam for 5 minutes, shaking the pan as you go. Remove the lid – the clams should have started to open (tap any that remain shut; if they still don't open discard them).

Put in the butter, add a grind of black pepper and stir through the clams and juices. Add the mint and toss through, then transfer the clams to serving bowls. Spoon the fried breadcrumbs and pistachios on top and serve.

Grilled Squid

with peas, mint, tomatoes and sweet vinegar

This may sound like an unusual combination but the hot, smoky, charred, straight-off-the-grill-squid set against the sweet-sour cooling fresh salad is a wondrous thing. I love this type of simple, big-flavoured cooking in the Mediterranean style. This dish whizzes me back to summers spent harbourside in Sicilian coastal towns, watching the daily catches come in, the fisherman firing up their little barbecues for lunch, the fresh seafood sizzling away … wonderful.

Fresh peas in season won't need pre-cooking, the acid in the vinegar will essentially cook them for you.

Serves 4

4 medium-sized squid, prepared and 'wing flaps' left on (a fishmonger will do this for you), with tentacles
70ml extra virgin olive oil
60ml sweet white wine vinegar (e.g. Chardonnay or moscatel vinegar)
1 teaspoon sugar, or to taste (optional)
120g podded fresh peas, or thawed frozen peas
a large handful of mint leaves

180g seasonal ripe vine tomatoes, 'eyes' removed and sliced into 1cm rounds
olive oil for cooking
1 teaspoon cumin seeds, lightly crushed
1 fresh red chilli, finely sliced
2 lemons, cut in half
sea salt and freshly ground black pepper

Turn the first squid upside down so that its wing flaps are flat on your chopping board. Push a large knife into the tube/body and leave the knife lying flat inside. With a sharp knife, slice the squid across as if you were going to cut it into rings. The knife that is lying inside will prevent you from cutting right through. You end up with a concertina effect with the squid sliced, but still holding together. Repeat with the other 3 squid.

Whisk together the extra virgin olive oil and vinegar. Add a little sugar if needed: the dressing should be sweet-sour.

Gently toss together the peas, three-quarters of the mint leaves and the tomatoes with the dressing. Season well. Leave to marinate while you cook the squid.

Prepare a barbecue or heat a ridged cast-iron grill pan to a medium heat. Rub the squid with olive oil, season well and sprinkle with the crushed cumin, ensuring this goes into the slits in the flesh that you've made.

Place the squid immediately on the hottest part of the barbecue grill or grill pan. Grill, turning every 30 seconds or so, or every time the squid starts to char, until the squid firm up and turn from opaque to white inside. This shouldn't take more than 5 minutes. Remove from the grill, sprinkle with the chilli and remaining mint, and serve with the tomato-pea salad on the side. I always grill lemon halves alongside to squeeze over the squid, and serve with my alioli (see page 283).

Stuffed Sardines
with almonds, anchovies, sultanas and preserved lemons

Traditionally *sarde a beccafico* are butterflied sardines stuffed with a mix of breadcrumbs, pine nuts, raisins and herbs, rolled up and baked between fresh bay leaves. The dish is named after a peculiar and prized species of bird, the *beccafico*, which feeds on wild figs and used to be hunted and consumed by the Sicilian aristocracy. The *beccafico* are replaced in this dish by sardines, the tails of which resemble that of the bird.

As with most regional Italian dishes, there are as many recipes for *sarde a beccafico* as there are Sicilian households. Indeed, every major Sicilian town seems to have a slightly different way of preparing them, either in the combination of ingredients or in the way the fish is stuffed and layered. My version is inspired by those found on the east of Sicily, where the Moorish influence is at its most pronounced. The sour preserved lemons add a gentle citric kick and combine well with the sweet raisins and the rich sardines.

Serves 4

800g very fresh sardines
extra virgin olive oil
50g panko breadcrumbs
25g sultanas, soaked in warm water
   to plump
20g preserved lemon, finely chopped
   (peel and all)
25g blanched almonds, chopped

1 tablespoon caster sugar
3 salted anchovies, finely chopped
4 tablespoons finely chopped flat-leaf
   parsley leaves
60ml freshly squeezed orange juice
fresh bay leaves
sea salt and freshly ground
   black pepper

Preparing the sardines is a fiddly task so it is best to ask your fishmonger to do it for you. Clean and scale the fish, then butterfly them, remove the heads and remove the spines/backbones, ensuring the tail is kept intact. Rinse the sardines under cold running water and pat dry.

Preheat the oven to 220°C/200°C fan/Gas Mark 7. Oil a baking dish with olive oil and set aside.

In a medium sauté pan set over a low heat, toast the breadcrumbs until golden and crisp, tossing them often to avoid burning. Transfer to a bowl and moisten with a generous drizzle of olive oil. Stir to dress evenly.

Drain the sultanas and squeeze dry, then roughly chop them. Add to the breadcrumbs together with the preserved lemon, almonds, sugar, anchovies, parsley and orange juice. Season well. Mix all the ingredients together to form a stuffing.

Place a small amount of stuffing over the flesh side of each sardine fillet. Roll up the fillets, starting from the head end. Arrange the rolled-up sardines, tail side up, in the greased baking dish, and tuck fresh bay leaves between them. Sprinkle any remaining stuffing over them, then drizzle with olive oil and season again. Bake the sardines for 25 minutes. Leave to cool for 10 minutes before serving.

Stuffed Whole Roasted Squid

with breadcrumbs, dried fruits, pine nuts, capers and fennel

This is a typical Sicilian coastal dish. The stuffing in the squid is packed with intense, punchy flavours that sing of the Mediterranean. Use fresh squid if available although a good-quality frozen squid will do nicely.

Serves 4

4 medium-sized squid (roughly 200g each), prepared
olive oil
100g fresh breadcrumbs
30g mixed raisins and sultanas, soaked in warm water to plump
20g capers plus 4 teaspoons of the brine

juice of 1 lemon
20g pine nuts, toasted
a large handful of fennel herb or dill, very roughly chopped
50g unsalted butter
sea salt and freshly ground black pepper

It's important that the inside of the squid tubes/bodies be nice and clean so double check this, then slice off about 1cm from the open end of each squid tube/body to make a neat entry. Place the squid tubes/bodies and tentacles on a cloth-lined tray and keep in the fridge until ready to stuff. They need to be dry for roasting so don't cover them – the air in the fridge will help them to dry out.

To make the stuffing, heat a medium saucepan over a medium heat and add a good amount of olive oil – about 1cm depth. When hot, fry the breadcrumbs, stirring as you go, until golden brown. Remove from the heat and stir in the drained raisins and sultanas, capers and brine, half of the lemon juice and the pine nuts. Season well. Finally, stir in most of the fennel herb, reserving a little to finish the dish. The stuffing should not be too dry – you should be able to mould it together – so add a splash of water if needed.

Now stuff the squid tubes/bodies: simply spoon in the stuffing mixture, pressing it in as you go so it's tightly packed. Fill each squid about three-quarters full. Secure the open end with a wooden cocktail stick to help seal in the stuffing.

Heat a large sauté pan over a medium heat and add a good lug of olive oil. When hot, place the stuffed squid in the pan and cook for 2 minutes on one side or until golden brown and caramelised. Turn them over, add the tentacles to the pan and cook for a further 2 minutes or until cooked through and golden brown. Turn them until browned on all sides.

Now add the butter and heat until it is foaming and lightly browned. Baste the squid with this, then add some seasoning, the remaining lemon juice and the rest of the fennel herb. Remove from the heat and leave to rest for 5 minutes before serving the squid with the buttery juices spooned over. I love to eat this with my Aeolian-style Summer Salad (see page 128).

Sicilian Octopus and Chickpea Stew
with salsa verde

Some of the best octopus in Sicily is to be found over the summer months, at the marina in Vila a Mare in Mondello. Little kiosks sell them served simply with lemon and sea salt. Delicious and very tender. Traditionally the octopus would have been bashed against the harbourside to tenderise them before slow cooking but now they are blast frozen and thawed, the process softening the meat perfectly.

This octopus recipe is one of my favourites and is inspired by my late-season visits to Mondello when the evenings become cooler and the octopus are cooked in a tomato stew with chickpeas. Wonderful when finished with some salsa verde (see page 280) and *pan grattato* (see page 287).

Serves 4–5

1 frozen octopus (1.5–1.8kg), thawed overnight in the fridge
5 bay leaves
1 onion, cut into quarters
3 garlic cloves, crushed
1 celery stick
1 teaspoon coriander seeds
4 plum tomatoes, 'eyes' removed and chopped
400g canned chopped tomatoes

400g canned chickpeas, drained and rinsed
1 tablespoon miniature capers
1 tablespoon chopped pitted green olives
extra virgin olive oil
salsa verde (see page 280)
pan grattato (see page 287), optional
sea salt and freshly ground black pepper

Place the octopus, bay leaves, onion, garlic, celery and coriander seeds in a large flameproof casserole and add enough water to cover the octopus. Set over a medium heat and bring to a simmer, then cook for about 1 hour 20 minutes or until the octopus is tender. A paring knife should pierce the octopus like butter. Remove from the heat and leave the octopus to cool fully in the liquid.

When cool, drain the liquid into a medium saucepan and bring to the boil. Reduce the liquid by about half.

Meanwhile, slice the head from the octopus and save for another use. Cut and separate the legs of the octopus for grilling.

When the cooking liquid has reduced add the fresh and canned tomatoes. Cook for 20 minutes or until the consistency is thick and rich. Now stir in the chickpeas, capers and olives and adjust the seasoning.

Prepare a barbecue or heat a ridged cast-iron grill pan to medium-high heat. Rub the octopus with olive oil, season and grill quickly for 2 minutes on each side of the tentacles to char. Remove the octopus from the grill and slice each tentacle into 3 or 4 pieces. Spoon out the chickpea stew. Top with the octopus and then the salsa verde and pan grattato, if using.

Baked Cod

with courgettes, rosemary, Marsala and brown crab

This is a one-pan dish that is very much more than the sum of its parts. Marsala has a natural affinity with cooking, akin to sherry in its fortified sweet or dry way, and fantastic with fish and shellfish. Here the Marsala is simply cooked down, blending with the brown crab and the rich mascarpone.

Courgettes are best in the spring and early summer when they have a denser, sweeter flesh.

Serves 4

50g brown crab meat
50g mascarpone
juice of ½ lemon
200g green courgettes, or mixed colour courgettes (green, yellow, white)
olive oil for cooking
2 garlic cloves, finely chopped

4 cod loin portions (about 200g each), skin removed
200ml dry Marsala
2 sprigs of rosemary, leaves picked
sea salt and freshly ground black pepper

Preheat the oven to 200°C/180°C fan/Gas Mark 6.

Whisk the brown crab meat with the mascarpone and some of the lemon juice, and season well.

Cut the courgettes in half lengthways and remove the seeds, then cut into bite-sized chunks. Spread out in a medium roasting tray. Season well, drizzle with olive oil and sprinkle over the garlic. Lay the pieces of cod on top, season them and drizzle with oil, then pour over the Marsala.

Place the tray in the oven and bake for 20 minutes or until the cod is lightly browned and just cooked through and the courgettes are tender.

Remove the cod and courgettes. Whisk the mascarpone-crab mix into the juices in the roasting tray and add the rosemary leaves. Set the tray over a low heat and simmer for 2–3 minutes. Season the sauce and add lemon juice to taste.

Serve the baked cod with the courgettes and crab sauce.

Grilled Monkfish
with fennel sausages, tomatoes and pumpkin

This robust recipe adopts the Spanish and Portuguese love of pairing meat and fish together within the same dish. It was inspired by a winter visit to Mazaro del Vallo, an important and busy fishing port on the island, which has some great cafés and restaurants nestled around the docks. Squid and dried pieces of salami were added together in a rich tomato casserole.

I find that monkfish is well suited to this style of hearty dish. I love it fresh from the grill with a lick of smoke.

Serves 4

2 fat pork and fennel sausages
(or pork sausages and a sprinkle
of fennel seeds)
olive oil for cooking
400g pumpkin or butternut squash,
peeled and diced into 2cm chunks
2 garlic cloves, finely chopped
2 teaspoons tomato paste
200ml red wine

50ml sweet red wine vinegar (e.g.
Cabernet Sauvignon vinegar)
300g ripe plum tomatoes, 'eyes'
removed and cut into pieces
200ml water
550g monkfish tail, cut into 4 portions
a handful of fennel fronds or dill
sea salt and freshly ground
black pepper

Remove the meat from the sausage casing and break into rough pieces.

Heat a medium flameproof casserole over a medium heat, add a lug of oil and, when hot, add the pumpkin pieces and sausage meat. (Add the fennel seeds now too, if using). Brown all over, then add the garlic and cook for 1 minute. Add the tomato paste and cook, stirring, for 1 minute or so. Pour in the wine and vinegar. Boil to reduce by half, then add the tomatoes and water. Turn down to a simmer and cook for 30–40 minutes or until reduced to a thick, rich sauce consistency. Remove from the heat and season. Leave to rest for 20 minutes, covered, while you cook the fish.

Prepare a barbecue or heat a ridged cast-iron grill pan to medium-high. Rub the monkfish with olive oil and season, then place on the barbecue or grill pan. Cook for 3–4 minutes on each side or until the fish is nicely charred and just cooked through. Remove and leave to rest for 3 minutes.

Check the seasoning of the sausage and tomato stew again and adjust if necessary, then stir in the fennel fronds or dill. Serve the monkfish on top.

I like this with my Swiss Chard Gratin with Ricotta, Mascarpone and Pine Nuts (see page 144).

Charcoal-grilled Tuna, Coriander Seeds, Lemon and Courgettes

A simple but beautiful dish inspired by a trip to Favignana, a little island off the west coast of Sicily. This is essentially an assembly of seasonal ingredients at their prime.

Tuna cooked over charcoal is a typical Mediterranean method of showcasing the meaty texture and beautiful flavours of the fish. Look for thick slices of tuna so that you can caramelise the outside whilst keeping the inside nice and pink and juicy.

Serves 4

2 small trombetta courgettes or small, firm green courgettes
olive oil for cooking
2 small garlic cloves, finely chopped
½ teaspoon dried chilli flakes
1 tablespoon coriander seeds, lightly crushed
100ml extra virgin olive oil
juice of ½ lemon

4 teaspoons sweet white wine vinegar (e.g. Chardonnay or moscatel vinegar)
4 thick slices of fresh tuna (each about 180–200g)
1 tablespoon picked oregano leaves
sea salt and freshly ground black pepper

If using the denser trombetta courgettes, just slice them into very thin rounds. If using regular courgettes, cut them in half lengthways and remove the seeds and fluffy centre, then cut the halves into very thin half-moons.

Prepare a barbecue (when it is ready for cooking the fish, the coals should have turned an ashen grey), or heat a ridged cast-iron grill pan to maximum.

Meanwhile, place a sauté pan over a medium heat and add a lug of olive oil, then add the garlic and the courgette slices. Season well and turn around in the pan before lowering the heat. Sprinkle with the chilli flakes and cook the courgettes for about 5 minutes or until tender. Remove from the heat and reserve.

Set a small sauté pan over a medium heat and tip in the crushed coriander seeds. Toast, tossing them occasionally, for 2–3 minutes or until they become fragrant. Remove from the heat and pour in the extra virgin olive oil, lemon juice and vinegar. Season. Set the dressing aside to infuse.

Season the tuna steaks and rub with oil, then place on the barbecue grill or hot grill pan. Cook for 2 minutes on each side or until nicely charred but still pink in the middle. Remove from the grill to a plate and spoon over a little of the coriander seed dressing. Leave to rest for a few minutes.

To serve, divide the courgettes among the plates and top with the tuna steaks. Stir the oregano leaves through the remaining dressing and spoon this over the fish. Delicious served with my Sweet and Sour Peppers on page 124.

Grilled Whole Mackerel
with spices, almond sauce and kale

There's a special joy to cooking fish on the bone. The flavour is intensified with the bones conducting the heat through the fish keeping it juicy and moist. This is a technique common in Mediterranean cookery but less so in the UK where fillets are often preferred. Mackerel isn't common in Sicily where you are more likely to find oily sardines or horse mackerel but when cooked like this over a grill at home you could be sitting outside a harbourside café somewhere on the west coast of the island watching the boats come in.

The spices here add both aromatic flavour and textural crunch.

Serves 4

300ml almond milk
a handful of Marcona almonds
½ garlic clove, finely chopped
4 teaspoons sweet white wine vinegar
   (e.g. moscatel or white balsamic
   vinegar)
4 small whole mackerel, gutted and
   fins trimmed
extra virgin olive oil for cooking

40g coriander seeds, lightly crushed
40g cumin seeds, lightly crushed
140g baby kale leaves, trimmed
juice of ½ lemon
60g sultanas, soaked in warm water
   to plump
40g pine nuts, lightly toasted
sea salt and freshly ground
   black pepper

Pour the milk into a saucepan, add the almonds and garlic, and bring slowly to the boil. Remove from the heat and rest for 10 minutes, then blitz in a blender to make a smooth purée. Season to taste, add the vinegar and reserve.

Lightly score the skin of each mackerel 4–5 times on both sides using a very sharp knife. Rub the fish with olive oil and season well.

Preheat the oven grill to maximum.

Place the mackerel on a baking tray and cook under the grill for 3 minutes on each side. Sprinkle over the spices and continue to cook for a minute or until the spices become fragrant. Remove from the heat and leave to rest for a few minutes in a warm spot.

Toss the kale leaves with the almond dressing, seasoning, lemon juice, drained sultanas and pine nuts. Leave for 5 minutes to macerate.

To serve, divide the dressed kale among the serving plates and top with the whole grilled mackerel.

Sea Bream
with almond and breadcrumb crust, vinegar and thyme

Sicilians love a coating of breadcrumbs on their fish (and meat) and in this recipe it not only gives a reassuring crunch but also ensures the fish is kept deliciously moist and juicy. The vinegar, traditionally a preservative to extend the shelf life of less than fresh fish, adds a lovely piquant flavour. Ensure the vinegar is of very good quality and use a sweeter variety such as a Chardonnay.

Serves 4

4 large sea bream fillets, skin lightly
   scored
100ml sweet white wine vinegar (e.g.
   Chardonnay or moscatel vinegar)
100g panko breadcrumbs
40g ground almonds

plain four for dusting
1 free-range egg, beaten
extra virgin olive oil for cooking
½ small handful of thyme
sea salt and freshly ground
   black pepper

Place the fish fillets in a bowl, season well and pour over about 75ml of the vinegar. Leave to marinate in the fridge for an hour.

Drain off the vinegar and dab the fillets dry. Mix the breadcrumbs with the ground almonds. Dredge the fillets in flour, then dip into the egg and coat with the breadcrumb-almond mix.

Heat a large sauté pan over a medium heat. Pour in olive oil for shallow frying – you'll need a good amount, perhaps 1cm in depth. When the oil is hot carefully lay the fish, skin side down, in the pan and fry for 3 minutes or until golden brown and crunchy. Turn the fish over, add the thyme sprigs and continue to fry for a further 2–3 minutes or until cooked through and golden brown.

Pour the remaining vinegar over the fish, then remove the fillets from the pan to drain on a kitchen towel. Serve hot with the thyme-infused oil and vinegar pan dressing spooned over.

The hot, crunchy bream fillets are delicious with the contrast of the Aeolian-style Summer Salad on page 128.

meat

Whilst the coastline of Sicily belongs to fish, the inland parts of the island belong to meat and to the crops.

Meat is a staple part of the in-lander's diet and livestock production represents one of the most important resources for the island's economy. Cattle, sheep and goats are the most prevalent and are mainly managed by small holders and pastoralists. Wild meats such as rabbit and deer are still hunted widely and enjoyed throughout the year.

Pork is very popular, and Sicily is famed for its black swine from the Nebrodi mountains. These semi-wild pigs are low in numbers, making them all the more desirable. Resembling more boar than pig, they roam freely, feeding from the oak forests in the north-west. The Nebrodi have many similarities to the Spanish iberico and the meat is equally as rich and just as delicious.

As in the rest of Italy, pork charcuterie is hugely popular. As soon as an animal is slaughtered parts of it will immediately be destined for preparation. Sicily's love of charcuterie was reborn in the eleventh century with the arrival of the Normans. Two centuries later, the prohibition of the consumption of pork was instigated by the Arabs and the traditions lapsed. Nowadays, centuries later, the Sicilian culinary melting pot is experienced most vividly through its varieties of coarse pork salamis featuring aromatic spicing from wild fennel, fennel pollen, black pepper, saffron, crushed coriander seeds, candied and dried fruits.

Horsemeat is still very popular on the island and considered a delicacy. I've tried it many times in various guises (much to my wife's dismay), the flavour being that of well-hung beef. It is often cooked as steaks and then drizzled with lemon and served in a bun, made up as meatballs and also prepared in the traditional *braciole* (see page 220).

Catania is the island capital of horsemeat and still has several specific horsemeat butchers who do a roaring trade in takeaway horse sandwiches. There are increasing calls for a ban on the eating of horsemeat and to reclassify horses as domestic animals. Whatever one's stance on what is a very controversial food issue, it's hard to deny that horsemeat is sustainable and healthy, the animals often being healthy retired riding horses.

The butcher's shops and markets of Sicily are filled to overflowing with all manner of animal cuts. You will usually find all the parts of the beast displayed on the counter, from the head to the tail and everything in between, with nothing wasted. The offal and extremities are seen by some as the choicest of cuts. I've included a couple of recipes in this chapter that use offal, including a meaty heart recipe (see page 201). Walk the street markets of Sicily and you'll see and smell grilling intestines and spleens, the aromas enticing eager locals to form hungry queues. Its undeniably hearty, full-on stuff and not for everyone, but as fast food goes it certainly beats MacDonald's.

Anatra all'Arrancia
roasted duck legs with blood orange sauce

In this dish I've used blood oranges to flavour a delicious, aromatic sauce to accompany crisp, fatty duck legs. The duck is lightly cured with salt and aromatics to add a flavour hit and draw out some of the moisture to help the duck roast and crisp to perfection.

Serves 4

4 large duck legs
8 sprigs of thyme
4 garlic cloves, roughly chopped
a 2cm piece of root ginger,
  peeled and grated
1 teaspoon crushed coriander seeds
100g coarse salt

5 blood oranges
olive oil for cooking
1 litre brown chicken stock
1 teaspoon unsalted butter
sea salt and freshly ground
  black pepper

Place the duck legs in a bowl along with the thyme, garlic, ginger, coriander seeds and coarse salt. Toss through well, then cover and transfer to the fridge to cure for 3 hours. This process will season the meat and also draw out some moisture, making it easier to roast.

Preheat the oven to 220°C/200°C fan/Gas Mark 7.

Remove the duck legs from the fridge. Rinse off the salt mix and pat dry.

Cut the oranges in half widthways. Slice the end off 4 of the halves so they will stand up straight.

Place the 4 trimmed orange halves on a roasting tray and sit the duck legs on top. Season the duck and drizzle with oil. Roast for 25 minutes to crisp and brown the skin, then turn down the oven temperature to 190°C/170°C fan/Gas Mark 5 and roast for a further 1 hour or until the legs are nice and tender and the oranges are soft and almost collapsing. Remove the duck legs and orange halves to a plate to rest.

Pour the fat from the roasting tray. Squeeze the juice from the remaining orange halves into the tray and set it over a high hob heat. Scrape to deglaze the pan, boiling to reduce the juice. Now add the stock and bring to the boil, then simmer for 20 minutes or so until you have a sauce-like consistency. Stir in the butter and season.

Serve the duck legs with the roasted orange halves and the sauce.

Whole Roast Chicken
stuffed with wild fennel, lemon leaves, garlic and bay

Wild fennel is the distant, roguish and more interesting cousin of what we know as fennel bulb, with an intense and exotic aniseed flavour and a wild, windswept aroma. The wild fennel is essentially a weed and grows everywhere, even in deepest darkest East London, where I live, although most people would walk past it without any idea of what its tender stalks and fronds can do for a dish. Sicilians, of course, have known its benefits for centuries and you'll find this foraged vegetable littered throughout the Sicilian culinary repertoire – in pasta with sardines, in risottos, with roasted porcetta or grilled fish, and stuffed into various vegetables, salamis and sausages. I urge you to find or pick it yourself – if unsuccessful in your quest then a very fresh baby fennel with plenty of fronds will do nicely!

Serves 5–6

a handful of wild fennel stalks and fronds, or a bunch of baby fennel bulbs
50g unsalted butter, at room temperature
1 whole chicken (1.7–2kg)
5 bay leaves

5 unsprayed lemon leaves
1 garlic bulb, cut in half crossways
4 banana shallots (unpeeled), cut in half lengthways
olive oil for cooking
sea salt and freshly ground black pepper

Preheat the oven to 220°C/200°C/Gas Mark 7. Cut the fennel fronds from the stalks (or any fronds from the baby fennel). Roughly chop the fronds, then whisk them into the softened butter. Season well.

Stuff the butter under the chicken's skin on its crown (the whole breast): carefully push your fingers flat under the skin (be careful not to break it), starting at the top of the crown and pushing gently down both sides to create a pocket on each side. Now push the fennel butter carefully into the pockets, using either your fingers or a small spoon, then push the skin back down in place. If there is any leftover butter, use it for something else.

Stuff the bay leaves, lemon leaves and half the garlic into the cavity of the chicken and season.

Place the shallots, the other garlic half and fennel stalks or baby fennel bulbs on a roasting tray (to act as a trivet). Set the chicken on top. Drizzle liberally with olive oil and season. Roast for 30 minutes or until the chicken skin is a lovely golden brown and has started to turn crisp.

Turn the oven down to 180°C/160°C fan/Gas Mark 4 and baste the chicken with the buttery juices, then continue roasting for 45–50 minutes or until the chicken is cooked through (the juices should run clear when a skewer is inserted into the thickest part of the crown).

Remove the chicken from the oven and leave to rest in a warm spot for 30 minutes before serving. This is a great Sunday roast alternative, and superb with my Fried Spinach, Courgette and Lemon Cakes on page 156.

Stuffed and Braised Lamb's Hearts
with broad beans and lemon

This is an intriguing recipe inspired by a rare winter visit to Taormina, the very civilised town on Sicily's east coast. One of my favourite restaurants on the island, Tischi Toshi, serves Sicilian classic dishes with a light touch and assured techniques. The dish I ate used a hefty ox heart and was served with creamy mashed potato. My version uses the lighter and smaller lamb's hearts and a pork stuffing flecked with vibrant green fava beans and lemon, the whole wrapped with fatty pancetta to lubricate the cooking process. Served hot, it's a robust winter dish and a great alternative to a roast; however you could also cook ahead and then cool to serve sliced with a fresh tomato salad, as is the Sicilian way.

Serves 4

2 lamb's hearts, prepared for cooking
   (a butcher will do this for you)
8–10 thin slices of pancetta (enough to
   cover the hearts)

For the stuffing
olive oil for frying
1 small onion, finely chopped
1 garlic clove, crushed
150g good-quality minced pork
100g broad beans (podded fresh or
   thawed frozen beans are both great
   – just remove the grey 'jackets'),
   roughly chopped

25g fresh white breadcrumbs
zest and juice of 1 unwaxed lemon
a handful of flat-leaf parsley, finely
   chopped
sea salt and freshly ground
   black pepper

For the braising liquid
1 onion, finely chopped
1 carrot, finely chopped
6 sprigs of thyme
4 bay leaves
350ml good-quality red wine
100ml balsamic vinegar

Preheat the oven to 180°C/160°C fan/Gas Mark 4.

First make the stuffing. Add a lug of olive oil to a hot sauté pan, then add the onion and cook until just soft. Add the garlic and cook for another minute or so. Remove from the heat to cool.

Combine the pork mince, broad beans, breadcrumbs, lemon zest and juice and about half of the parsley in a large mixing bowl. Add the cooked onion and garlic. Season and mix well.

Pat dry the lamb's hearts with kitchen paper, then stuff the cavities with the pork mixture, packing it in firmly. Wrap the pancetta around the hearts to cover them completely. You can secure the parcels with butcher's string if you like. Set aside.

For the braising liquid, heat a flameproof casserole (with a lid) on the hob, splash in some oil and, when it's hot, add the onion and carrot. Cook gently until they've softened.

...continued on page 202

Meanwhile, take the sauté pan you cooked the onion for the stuffing in and heat it with a lug of olive oil. Sear the hearts in the hot oil, browning each side in turn. When they're browned all over, transfer them to the casserole, placing them on top of the vegetables. Sprinkle over the thyme, bay leaves and the rest of the parsley.

Deglaze the sauté pan with a splash of the red wine, scraping the bottom well. Tip the deglazed juices over the hearts, then pour the remaining wine into the casserole. Place the lid on the pot and transfer to the oven to cook for about 2 hours or until the hearts are tender and the wine has reduced to a saucy consistency.

When the cooking time is almost up, heat a clean frying pan, add the balsamic vinegar and cook gently until it reduces to a syrup (you'll have about 2 tablespoons).

Remove the hearts from the casserole, wrap them in foil and leave them to rest while you finish the sauce. Strain the cooking liquor from the casserole into a saucepan, pressing the vegetables to extract as much flavour as possible before discarding them. Stir the syrupy balsamic vinegar into the strained cooking liquor. If there's a layer of fat on top of the liquid, skim it off with a spoon. Place the saucepan on the hob and bubble to reduce the liquid by half. Season to taste.

Cut each heart in half lengthways, spoon over the liquor and serve.

Lamb Tartare
with chilli, capers, pine nuts and mint

Though raw chopped lamb is eaten as a staple in the Middle East, most commonly in the dish of *kibbeh nayeh* where it is mixed with fresh herbs and bulgur wheat, it is less common in Europe. I have, however, tried a Sicilian-style lamb tartare in a restaurant in Palermo, the lamb mixed with raisins and grilled onions, but the lamb flavour was overly powerful and in need of tempering. My version, fresh and zingy, includes some simple but delicious lamb fat toast – essential for scooping up the tartare.

Serves 4 as antipasti

400g very fresh lamb rump, fat removed and reserved
extra virgin olive oil
1 banana shallot, finely chopped
50g capers, finely chopped
25g Dijon mustard
1 fresh red chilli, deseeded and finely chopped
a small handful of mint leaves

1 tablespoon toasted pine nuts, roughly chopped
2 teaspoons Worcestershire sauce
a few drops of Tabasco
12 slices of ciabatta (2cm thick)
alioli (see page 283) to serve
sea salt and freshly ground black pepper

Place the reserved lamb fat in a small saucepan with a few lugs of extra virgin olive and set over a very low heat. You want to slowly render (melt) the fat to a liquid that will mix with the oil. Set the fat aside.

Trim any sinew from the lamb rump. Using a very sharp knife, cut the lamb into tiny dice. Try not to mash the meat – you want clean neat cubes. Place the lamb in a cold mixing bowl and add the shallot, capers, mustard, chilli, half the mint leaves, half the pine nuts, Worcestershire sauce and Tabasco. Season well, then mix until everything is evenly incorporated. Taste to check the seasoning and adjust to your liking. Cover and chill.

Preheat the oven grill.

Brush the lamb fat and olive oil mix over both sides of each bread slice, then toast under the hot grill until golden brown. Season.

Serve the tartare, fridge cold, sprinkled with the remaining pine nuts and mint and with the warm toasts on the side. I like to serve this with a punchy, garlicky alioli.

Sweet and Sour Rabbit

on toast

A perfect dish for both winter and summer months, that can be served either at room temperature in the sweltering heat, as the Sicilians do (the sweet and sour is actually very refreshing) or piping hot on a cold winter's day.

Rabbits have historically been associated with peasant food and this dish typifies the Sicilian style, the mixture of sweet and sour adding intense flavour but also preservation. A whole chicken of roughly the same size and jointed in the same way would be a perfect substitute for the rabbit.

Serves 4

1 whole rabbit (about 1.2kg), skinned and jointed, with its offal (a butcher will prepare the rabbit for you)
olive oil for cooking
1 red onion, finely sliced
1 carrot, finely sliced
5 ripe cherry tomatoes, quartered
1 fresh red chilli, halved lengthways and deseeded
5 fresh bay leaves
50g pine nuts

50g blanched almonds
½ teaspoon ground cloves
1 cinnamon stick
4 pared strips of orange zest
150ml full-bodied Sicilian red wine
350ml water
100ml thick balsamic vinegar
1 tablespoon runny honey
4 slices of sourdough bread
sea salt and freshly ground black pepper

Place the rabbit joints and offal in a cold flameproof casserole and add 3 tablespoons of oil. Set the casserole on a medium-high heat and brown the rabbit, turning occasionally. Add the onion, carrot, tomatoes, chilli, bay leaves, pine nuts, almonds, cloves, cinnamon and orange zest. Pour in the wine and water. Bring to the boil, then simmer on a low heat for 15 minutes.

Pour in the balsamic and add the honey. Cook, stirring occasionally, for a further 30 minutes or until the rabbit is very tender and the liquid has reduced to a dark, thick, flavourful coating sauce. Check the seasoning. Remove from the heat and leave the stew to rest for 10 minutes.

Meanwhile, fry the slices of sourdough bread in olive oil until golden brown on both sides.

Place a slice of toast on each plate. Arrange the rabbit on top and spoon over the delicious rich juices, which will soak into and soften the bread.

Sicilian Pork and Fennel Sausage
with red wine, grapes and honey

Sicily's pork *salsicca*, usually sold in long thin spiral rings, similar to a Cumberland sausage ring, are characterised by their coarse cut texture and the addition of fennel seeds. They are one of the most delicious things cooked over a charcoal or wood-fired barbecue.

During the summer months in Palermo vendors set up rickety little grills along the streets cooking them in the heat of the midday sun, filling the air with smoke and the aroma of charred pork and fennel. If you don't want to grill or barbecue your *salsicca* then this recipe comes a close second, the rich wine, honey and grapes cooking down with the tasty pork fat to make the most delicious sauce.

A good Italian deli or butcher will be able to source fennel sausages or even make them for you.

Serves 4

a 1kg pork and fennel sausage
(preferably in a ring)
olive oil for cooking
500ml red Nero d'Avola wine

1 tablespoon runny honey
4 sprigs of rosemary, leaves picked
100g black seedless grapes, cut in half
lengthways

Heat a medium sauté pan over a medium heat. Brush the sausage with oil, then carefully lay it in the pan, ensuring the ring fits in and evenly covers the bottom. Cook for 2 minutes or so until the base is golden brown and beginning to crisp up. Turn the ring over and cook for a further 2 minutes. Pour in the wine and honey and sprinkle over the rosemary and grapes. Continue to cook until the sausage is cooked through, reducing the wine as you go until syrupy and rich. The grapes will soften and start to break down a little.

Transfer the sausage to a serving plate and spoon over the rich wine and grape sauce.

This is brilliant with my Sweet and Sour Peppers on page 124 and some Focaccia on page 22.

Stuffed Aubergines
with pork, pine nuts, rice and ricotta

These delicious ragù-stuffed aubergine boats are ideal served straight from the oven, but they are also great served cold. In the Sicilian summer months you'll see the locals eating this type of thing, wrapped in foil and served from a food cooler or picnic hamper on the beach. It's the ultimate picture dish, and similar in some ways to the British scotch egg or pork pie. Just prepare the recipe as below, cool and then transfer to the fridge until ready to eat.

Serves 4

2 medium-sized aubergines
olive oil for cooking
100g minced pork
1 garlic clove, finely chopped
2 salted anchovies, finely chopped
200ml red wine
200g canned chopped tomatoes
100g basmati rice, cooked and cooled

a handful of flat-leaf parsley,
    finely chopped
50g ricotta cheese
20g Parmesan cheese, finely grated
zest of ½ unwaxed lemon
30g pine nuts, lightly toasted
sea salt and freshly ground
    black pepper

Preheat the oven to 190°C/170°C fan/Gas Mark 5.

Cut the aubergines in half lengthways, keeping the ends intact. Scoop out some of the flesh from each half with a spoon, leaving about a 1cm layer of flesh. Chop the scooped-out flesh into 1cm dice.

Lay the aubergine halves on an oven tray cut side up. Season and drizzle with oil. Roast for 20 minutes or until just cooked through and lightly browned. Remove from the oven to cool.

Heat a medium flameproof casserole over a medium heat and add a lug of olive oil. When hot, add the pork mince and season. Cook for a few minutes to brown all over. Remove the mince from the pan using a slotted spoon and reserve. In the oil left in the pan, fry the scooped-out aubergine flesh with the garlic until golden brown. Season well and stir through the anchovies.

Return the cooked mince to the pan. Add the wine and boil until it has all but evaporated. Add the tomatoes, bring back to a simmer and cook for 20 minutes or so until thickened and rich. Stir in the cooked rice and parsley and season well, then cook for 2 minutes. Add a little water if the mix is too thick. Remove from the heat and cool.

Divide the mince-rice mix among the 4 aubergine halves. Crumble over the ricotta and sprinkle on the Parmesan. Bake for 20 minutes or until piping hot and bubbling and the cheese has melted. Finish with the lemon zest and pine nuts and serve. Delicious with va topping of pan grattato (see page 287).

Pork, Chilli and Marjoram Polpette
cooked with lemon and lemon leaves

I love the fresh and fragrant style of *polpette*, or *purpette* in the Sicilian dialect. It's all about the interaction between the lemon and lemon leaves and the rich juicy pork and the heady aroma of fresh marjoram. I make the meatballs larger than expected to retain their juiciness – they also look great with a thin slice of lemon draped over the top. Lemon leaves add another level of flavour. The leaves are abundant in Sicily but harder to source in the UK – you'll have to ask your friendly grocer for help.

Meatballs are traditionally eaten at a Sunday lunch in Sicily where the remaining sauce from the pan is then tossed with pasta for a delicious but frugal Sunday night supper. Try it.

Serves 4

600g quality minced pork with a good
    fat content
2 tablespoons grated Parmesan cheese
70g fresh white breadcrumbs
1 fresh red chilli, deseeded and
    finely chopped
½ handful of marjoram, leaves picked
a handful of flat-leaf parsley leaves,
    finely chopped
1 free-range egg, beaten

2–3 unwaxed lemons
extra virgin olive oil for cooking
200ml white wine
500ml chicken stock
40g unsalted butter
a handful of unsprayed lemon
    leaves (optional)
sea salt and freshly ground
    black pepper

Preheat the oven to 200°C/180°C fan/Gas Mark 6.

Place the pork in a bowl and season well. Stir in the Parmesan, breadcrumbs, chilli, marjoram, parsley and egg. Mix well, then add the zest and juice of ½ lemon. Mix well again. Shape into 12 large meatballs. Place in the fridge to firm.

Carefully slice 12 thin rounds from the remaining lemons to drape over the meatballs. Remove the meatballs from the fridge.

Heat a large flameproof casserole over a medium heat and add a lug of oil. When hot add the meatballs and brown them on all sides. Transfer the meatballs to a plate, top with the slices of lemon and secure each with a wooden cocktail stick.

Pour the wine into the casserole and turn up the heat. Scrape the bottom of the pot to deglaze, then boil to reduce somewhat. Add the stock and butter. Return the meatballs to the pan. Bring the stock to a simmer and add the lemon leaves, if using.

Cover the pot and place in the oven to cook for 35 minutes or until the polpette are cooked through and the sauce is rich and tasty. Season to taste, then leave to rest for 10 minutes before serving.

Roasted Pork Belly
with fennel and sticky quinces

Belly is my favourite cut of pork. Crispy skin, unctuous, melting layers of meat and the deep flavours of the fat that bastes and brings everything together. Fennel is a classic Sicilian accompaniment to pork – on the island it will likely be the spindly wild fennel found growing all over. Fennel's herby-aniseed flavours are just the thing for the rich pork. The quince adds the sweet and sour element you would normally find with apple but with an added lovely, ambrosial depth. This is my ideal Sicilian-style winter Sunday lunch.

Serves 4

2 small quinces, halved and cored
25g caster sugar
5 bay leaves
2 fennel bulbs, each cut into quarters
   lengthways
1 garlic bulb, cut in half crossways
a 1kg piece of pork belly, skin scored

1 teaspoon fennel seeds
olive oil for cooking
100ml honey
½ bottle white wine
sea salt and freshly ground
   black pepper

Put the quinces in a saucepan, cover with water (about 500ml) and add the sugar. Bring to the boil, then simmer for about 1 hour or until just tender. Reserve.

Preheat the oven to its highest temperature, around 250°C/230°C fan/Gas Mark 10.

Place the bay leaves, fennel quarters and garlic halves in a roasting tray. Place the pork on top, skin side up. Season well, sprinkle on the fennel seeds and drizzle with a little oil. Roast for 25–30 minutes or until the skin (crackling) has browned and is very crispy.

Turn down the oven heat to 200°C/180°C fan/Gas Mark 6. Place the drained poached quince in the roasting tray, drizzle around the honey and pour around the wine. Cook for a further 1 hour or until the pork is very tender, and the wine, honey and meat juices have reduced to a lovely, rich, sticky consistency.

If the pork still needs more cooking and the juices have reduced too much, then just add a glass of water and continue cooking.

When ready, remove from the oven and leave to rest for 20 minutes before serving.

Grilled Bavette

with braised courgettes, mint, chilli and gremolata

This simple technique for cooking the courgettes harnesses their natural flavours, unlike roasting where their natural freshness can be lost. I use dense-fleshed sweeter varieties with less water content. This mint-chilli combination is a perfect partner for courgette.

You could use any cut of grilling-beef you like, but I prefer the flavour and texture of the economical bavette, commonly used all over Sicily and Europe.

Serves 4

800g beef bavette, cut into 4 steaks
100ml extra virgin olive oil
1 large, fresh red chilli, deseeded and
　finely chopped
3 garlic cloves, finely sliced
2 teaspoons fennel seeds,
　lightly crushed
70ml balsamic vinegar
½ handful of mint, leaves picked
　and stalks kept

olive oil for cooking
50g unsalted butter
4 heavy-fleshed courgettes (Italian
　varieties such as Romano or
　Grezzina or a British-grown variety),
　very finely sliced
juice of ½ lemon
1 quantity gremolata (see page 281)
sea salt and freshly ground
　black pepper

Place the steaks in a bowl and drizzle over the extra virgin olive oil. Season well and add half of the chilli, half of the garlic, the fennel seeds, balsamic and the stalks from the mint. Massage the meat with the marinade, then cover and leave to marinate for at least 3 hours or overnight.

Prepare a barbecue or heat a ridged cast-iron grill pan to medium heat.

Place a large sauté pan over a medium heat and add a lug of olive oil and the butter. When hot add the remaining garlic and chilli and soften gently before adding the courgette slices. Season well, then cook the courgettes gently but quickly until softened and still green. Add the mint leaves and lemon juice and reserve.

Drain the beef from the marinade and season, then place on the barbecue grill or hot grill pan. Cook for 3–4 minutes on each side or until the surface is caramelised; the meat will be pink inside. Leave to rest in a warm spot for 5 minutes.

Arrange the courgettes on plates. Slice the steaks into thin slices and place on top. Spoon over the gremolata and serve.

Braised Tripe Ragusa-style

I couldn't write a Sicilian cookbook without *trippa* making an appearance! Tripe is considered a delicacy in Sicily, along with most other offal, and you'll see it almost everywhere – in restaurants, in cafés and from street food vendors. It is an acquired taste and requires careful washing, cleaning and soaking prior to cooking in order to remove as much of the farmyard from it as possible.

This is an old recipe from Ragusa. I love it. The sauce and the cheese helping to temper the tripe's natural funky flavour. Serve it with the stuffed tomatoes on page 154.

Serves 4

1 tablespoon blanched almonds
1 tablespoon blanched hazelnuts
1kg calf's tripe (prepared by your butcher)
extra virgin olive oil for cooking
500ml chicken stock (quality shop-bought or home-made)
5 bay leaves
10 black peppercorns

1 large aubergine, cut into 1cm slices lengthways
4 tablespoons finely grated caciocavallo or Parmesan cheese
a pinch of ground cinnamon
a handful of oregano leaves
sea salt and freshly ground black pepper

Preheat the oven to 200°C/180°C fan/Gas Mark 6.

Spread the almonds and hazelnuts on a small baking tray and toast in the oven for 8 minutes or until they just start to turn golden brown. Remove from the oven and cool, then roughly chop.

Cut the tripe into 1cm strips and season well.

Heat a large sauté pan over a medium heat, add a lug of oil and sear the tripe strips until well coloured. Now add the stock, bay leaves and peppercorns and bring to a simmer. Cook gently for an hour or so until the tripe is very tender. The stock will have reduced by about two-thirds.

While the tripe is cooking, fry the aubergine slices in some oil in a sauté pan over a medium heat until cooked through and golden brown on both sides. Season and drain well.

Add the aubergine slices to the tripe along with the caciocavallo or Parmesan, toasted nuts and cinnamon. Stir everything together over a low heat and check the seasoning, then sprinkle over the oregano. Serve.

Veal Braciole
stuffed with 'nduja, raisins and pine nuts

Braciole is a perfect example of the frugal and witty nature of Sicilian cuisine. Thin slices of meat are rolled and stuffed with a filling such as breadcrumbs, salami or cheese and then herbs, allowing the meat to go further whilst also creating a delicious and intelligent dish.

Braciole come in many guises; my version uses rose veal, but you could use beef or pork. I like to stuff mine with a salty pecorino, breadcrumbs, thyme and some spicy pork pâté – here I'm using Calabrian 'nduja. I also add some distinctly Moorish flavours with pine nuts and raisins. Traditionally these would be fried in olive oil, but I like to add some smokiness and cook them over a grill or barbecue.

Serves 4–6

8 x 100g pieces of rose veal loin
25g toasted pine nuts
30g raisins
25g capers
60g fresh breadcrumbs
olive oil
100g 'nduja (Calabrian pork pâté),
  softened at room temperature

75g pecorino cheese, grated
a handful of thyme leaves
200ml tomato sauce (see page 286)
sea salt and freshly ground
  black pepper

Each piece of veal needs to be pounded to about 5mm thickness. A butcher might do this for you but if not here's how: place a piece of veal between 2 pieces of clingfilm and bash the meat with a kitchen hammer or the back of a sturdy saucepan – all over so as to get an even surface. Be careful not to rip the meat. Repeat until you have 8 flat pieces of meat, then put them into the fridge.

In a food processor pulse/blitz together the pine nuts, raisins, capers and breadcrumbs with a good lug of olive oil to form a rough paste.

Lay out the pieces of veal on a work surface and divide the 'nduja among them. Spread the 'nduja over the veal in a thin layer, leaving a 1cm clear border around the edge. Spread a layer of the caper/pine nut paste over the 'nduja, then sprinkle with pecorino and thyme leaves. Roll up each piece of veal to form a neat parcel and secure with a wooden cocktail stick.

Prepare a barbecue or heat a ridged cast-iron grill pan to medium. Brush the veal rolls with oil and season well. Cook for about 3 minutes on each side or until cooked through and nicely browned and smoky.

Leave to rest for 5 minutes before serving, with the warm fresh tomato sauce on the side.

Charcoal-grilled Venison Haunch
with grape must, juniper and sauté greens

Grape must or *saba* is a reduced grape juice which includes skin, pips and all – in effect the first stage in the wine making process. Sweet-sour and syrupy and without alcohol. Delicious in many things from vinaigrettes to desserts flavourings. I particularly love its marinating qualities as it naturally tenderises and imparts a delicious fruity tang to stronger flavoured meats such as game and beef. This is great on a barbecue as the marinade caramelises to a sticky crust over the fire. A hot griddle will do fine as an alternative.

Serves 4

a 1kg boned venison haunch, sinew removed (a thick piece is better for cooking on a barbecue)
1 teaspoon juniper berries, crushed
1 teaspoon dried oregano or marjoram leaves
500ml saba (grape must)

olive oil for cooking
150g seasonal greens (I recommend strong, bitter flavours to match the strong meat, such as chard, kale or large leaf spinach), trimmed
sea salt and freshly ground black pepper

Place the venison in a bowl, season well and rub with the juniper and the dried herbs. Pour over the grape must and massage well into the meat, then pour in enough water to cover the venison completely. Cover and leave to marinate in the fridge for 8 hours, turning the venison once or twice as you go.

About 30 minutes before cooking, remove the venison from the marinade (reserving the marinade) and leave to come up to room temperature. Prepare a barbecue or set a ridged cast-iron grill pan on a medium heat.

Season the venison and drizzle with a little oil, then place on the hot grill or pan. Cook for 6 minutes on one side to caramelise, then turn over and continue cooking to brown the other side. Every time the meat is turned, use a pastry brush to lightly apply some of the marinade.

When all sides of the venison are caramelised (a thick piece of meat will need to be browned on 4 sides), move it to a cooler spot on the barbecue or reduce the heat under the grill pan. Continue cooking but without too much further colouring, turning and basting regularly, until the meat is medium rare with an internal temperature of 63°C – about 25 minutes in total (cook for 5 minutes longer for medium or 10 minutes more for medium to well done). When the meat is cooked, transfer to a plate, and brush liberally with more of the marinade, then leave to rest in a warm spot.

While the meat is resting, heat a large sauté pan over a medium heat, add a lug of oil and throw in the greens. Season well, stir and cook for a few minutes or until wilted. Pour the remaining marinade into a small pan and bring to the boil.

Slice the venison into thick pieces and serve with the hot greens and with the marinade and juices poured over.

sweets

From the zingy, palate-tingling ices made from the island's luscious lemons and tangerines to the vivid green and garish Cassata Siciliana, Sicilian cakes, desserts and sweets are steeped in history, romance and excess.

It was the Arabs that first brought sugarcane to Sicily and with it the sweet tooth that so defines the islanders' tastebuds. The use of honey, which had been previously used for sweet treats, began to dwindle with the arrival of sugarcane. And then when sugar was combined with the island's array of nuts, a whole new wonderful range of confections were developed and eagerly devoured. Examples are many, far too many to mention, but perhaps one of the most famous confections and a personal favourite are the delicious almond biscuits, *pasta di mandorla*. I love them and if seen on a market stall or shop window should be bought and enjoyed with alacrity and without any hesitation.

Ask anyone who's been to Sicily about the *dolci* and they are likely to wax lyrical about the *cannoli* – the fried crisp tubes stuffed with ricotta and a variety of flavourings such as candied fruits, saffron and pistachio. *Cannoli* are a direct descendant from the Arabic Quanwat, a fried and stuffed pastry tube. *Cannoli* are indulgent and naughty, in all the right ways. If you are on a search for the ultimate *cannoli* then visit the wonderful Laboratorio Pasticceria Roberto situated on a quiet back street in Taormina. Roberto has some of the best *cannoli* and *dolci* I've ever tried.

As with so much of Sicily's food, many of the island's best-known pastries were born out of poverty and necessity. *Sfinci*, or fried dough, is just that. Originally it would have been a spartan mix of pig's fat and coarse flour, fried in more pork fat and then drizzled with honey. Brutalist cooking but something sweet to eat at the end of the day. It is still a popular street food and festival treat, although nowadays with a lighter dough, fried in vegetable oil and dusted with icing sugar, perhaps stuffed with cream or custard.

There is also *pignoccata*, little fried balls of dough, again drenched in honey and then sprinkled with multi-coloured sugar confetti: the simple 'elevated' to celebratory with its garish crunchy coating. And then there are Sicily's popular rice fritters (my version is on page 246) which were created by the Benedictine monks in a time of hardship as a way to use leftover rice, the cooked rice then bound in sweetened milk, fried and scented with orange flower water. A frugal sweet treat still popular to this day.

In the early sixteenth century chocolate found its way into the salons of Europe as the drink of choice amongst the monied and landed classes. It was only much later though, that chocolate as a confection and as a flavouring for savoury dishes made its mark on the island's cuisine, where it now holds court in a wide variety of delicious forms and culinary constructs.

I remember my first visit to Palermo and a wonderful afternoon spent in a sugary haze at the city's most famous café, Spinatto. Forget any other pastry shop you've ever experienced – this Sicilian grande dame is an assault on the senses with banks of multi-coloured, multi-textured cakes, pastries, fired pastries, various *cannoli*, bejewelled sweets and candied fruits. Then there's the frozen section – *gelato*, *granite* (served in fluffy brioche buns), frozen *gelato* cakes, ice cream sandwiches and *semifreddo*. There's a kitsch beauty in the garishness and I was captivated for an hour or more, eyeing up the fridge counters and freezers before ordering a ricotta and orange *cannoli*, a brioche bun with pistachio ice cream and a rum baba with Marsala cream and wild strawberries, all washed down with a strong black coffee.

I looked around the café, full of Sicilian families and friends on a Sunday afternoon, and realised that Sicilian *dolci* are a culture within a culture. There are as many different pastries and sweets as there are saints' days in Sicily and as many versions of one cake as there are regions. It is my quest to try them all.

Baci Panteschi

kissing biscuits

A simple peasant shepherd wished to give an indulgent gift to a loved one, but without funds he had to be creative and so the *bacio pantesco* was born. Delicious both hot and cold, crunchy and soft, savoury and sweet. And for complete authenticity you could buy the special flower-shaped *baci* iron that gives the 'biscuits' their unique shape.

Serves 6–8

350ml full-fat milk
1½ teaspoons dried yeast
300g plain flour, sifted
a pinch of fine sea salt
4 large free-range eggs
1.5 litres groundnut oil for frying
icing sugar for dusting

For the filling
300g sheep's milk ricotta
2 tablespoons caster sugar
zest of ½ orange

Make the filling first. Mix the ricotta with the caster sugar and orange zest. Reserve in the fridge.

Warm 50ml of the milk and dissolve the yeast in this. Leave for a few minutes to ferment and bubble. Now make the batter. Whisk together the flour, salt, eggs, remaining milk and the yeast mixture. Leave to rest for 10 minutes.

Heat the oil in a deep-fat fryer or deep saucepan to 180°C (a little batter dropped in will fizzle and brown on impact with the oil).

Plunge the baci iron into the hot oil, then immediately into the batter. Put the iron back into the oil and fry for about a minute or until the fritter slips off into the oil. When the fritter swells and turns golden brown it is ready. Remove with tongs or a slotted spoon and drain on kitchen paper. Keep warm.

Repeat until all the batter is used. Spoon some of the ricotta filling on to a baci and sandwich with another. Douse liberally with icing sugar and serve. Excellent with a glass of limoncello.

Buccellati
black fig, almond and cinnamon biscuits

Known as *cucciddati*, or *cucidati*, *buccellati* are Sicily's best-known traditional Christmas celebration biscuits. A thin pastry wrapped around a filling of dried black figs, nuts and spices, they are reminiscent of the sticky fig biscuits we had as children – but better. They can be glazed and decorated with coloured sprinkles or simply dusted with icing sugar and then given as Christmas presents to family and friends. One Christmas at Norma I decided I'd get the team to make *buccellati* as a festive giveaway for our guests – they were so popular I had to employ a part time commis chef for two weeks to keep up with the demand.

I've made *buccellati* at other times of year too (a sacrilege, I know) but Christmas is only once a year and they are so delicious. Omit the decorative stage at the end for a lighter version.

Makes 40–45

For the filling
500g dried black figs
120g blanched almonds
35g green pistachios
150g raisins
35g pine nuts
125g runny honey
200g orange marmalade
zest of 2 oranges
a pinch of ground cinnamon

For the dough
180g plain flour
180g icing sugar

2 teaspoons baking powder
a pinch of fine sea salt
200g chilled butter or lard, diced
3 free-range eggs plus 1 yolk,
    beaten together

For the glaze (optional)
2 free-range egg whites
310g icing sugar, sifted
1–2 tablespoons finely chopped
    pistachios or coloured sprinkles

To decorate (optional)
icing sugar for dusting

Put the figs into a bowl and pour boiling water over them. Leave for at least 15 minutes to soften, then drain. Remove the stems with a knife before chopping roughly. Place in a food processor and blitz until you have a paste, then transfer to a bowl.

Place the almonds and pistachios in the food processor and chop quite finely, leaving them a little rough; don't go so far as to turn them into a paste too. Add to the figs along with the rest of the filling ingredients. Combine well. Chill in the fridge for a couple of hours at least, preferably overnight, so the flavours can develop.

For the dough, place the first 4 ingredients in a bowl. Rub in the butter (or pulse in a food processor) until the mixture resembles breadcrumbs. Add the eggs and mix in to make a smooth dough. If it is a little too sticky, add a bit more flour. If it's dry or crumbly, add some cold water, a little at a time, until it comes together. Wrap the dough firmly in clingfilm and put into the fridge to rest and chill – at least 1 hour but better overnight.

...continued on page 232

Preheat the oven to 200°C/180°C fan/Gas Mark 6. Line 1–2 baking trays with baking parchment.

It helps if both the dough and the filling are chilled, so shape the biscuits in batches. Cut the chilled dough into 4–6 smaller portions and work with one portion at a time (keeping the others wrapped in clingfilm in the fridge). Divide the filling into 4–6 portions and keep chilled.

Roll the first portion of dough into a sausage shape, then flatten and roll out on a lightly floured surface to a long rectangle, no more than 3mm thick. Place a portion of filling along the middle of the rectangle lengthways in a long, thin log shape, no more than 2.5cm wide. Roll up the dough sheet around the filling to enclose completely, overlapping the ends of the dough sheet just a little bit. Trim off the extra dough (this is rather like making a sausage roll). Roll the log gently back and forth on the work surface with the palms of your hands to seal the edges, and tighten and lengthen the log ever so slightly. Cut the log across into 7.5cm pieces, cutting diagonally.

Place the pieces on the baking tray and bake for 15–20 minutes or until the pastry is just beginning to turn golden. Remove from the oven and cool on a wire rack. Once all the biscuits have been baked, leave the oven on.

While the biscuits are baking and cooling, prepare the glaze (if using). With a fork, beat the egg whites until they become frothy. Add the icing sugar and mix until you have a smooth mixture with the consistency of honey. Add more sugar if it is not thick enough (if necessary, you can pass the mixture through a sieve to make it perfectly smooth).

Spoon or brush the glaze over the top of each biscuit, then if you like top each with a pinch of chopped pistachios or coloured sprinkles. Place the biscuits back on the baking tray and return to the oven to bake for a further 5 minutes or until the glaze feels dry and set. Cool completely before serving.

Alternatively, rather than glazing you could simply dust the biscuits with icing sugar.

Cannoli

with ricotta, candied fruits and chopped pistachios

The original for this recipe featured in my last book *Moorish*, albeit with a saffron ricotta filling. However, I had to include a recipe for *cannoli* in *Sicilia* as they are the most iconic of Sicilian sweet treats and a personal favourite.

I've eaten my fair share of *cannoli* travelling through Sicily and have developed a recipe for them at Norma. Our customers love them – one with a coffee at the end of the meal and one to take home in a specially designed Norma *cannoli* gift box.

As the *cannoli* are deep-fried, you'll need a special *cannoli* tube to get the authentic look – they are widely available to buy.

Makes about 28

For the pastry shells
375g plain flour
4 tablespoons caster sugar
1 teaspoon ground cinnamon
¼ teaspoon fine sea salt
45g unsalted butter
2 free-range eggs, beaten
1 tablespoon dry Marsala
2 tablespoons distilled malt vinegar
2 tablespoons cold water
1 egg white for sealing
500ml vegetable oil for frying

For the filling
750g ricotta cheese
250g icing sugar
2 teaspoons vanilla extract
120g finely diced candied fruits
30g green pistachios, very finely chopped
40g icing sugar for dusting

First make the pastry dough. In a medium bowl, mix together the flour, sugar, cinnamon and salt. Cut in the butter until it is in pieces no larger than peas. Make a well in the centre and pour in the eggs, Marsala, vinegar and water. Mix with a fork until the dough becomes stiff, then finish mixing by hand, kneading on a clean surface. Add a bit more water if needed to bring the dough together. Knead for about 10 minutes, then cover and chill for 1 hour.

Divide the cannoli dough into thirds and work with one piece at a time. For each batch, flatten the dough just enough to get it through a pasta machine. Roll the dough through successively thinner settings until you have reached the thinnest one. (If you don't have a pasta machine, roll out the dough using a floured rolling pin as thinly and evenly as possible.) Dust lightly with flour, if necessary.

...continued on page 234

Place the sheets of dough on a lightly floured surface. Using a large glass or bowl, cut out 10–12.5cm circles. Dust the circles with a light coating of flour (this will help you later in removing the shells from the tubes). Roll each dough circle around a cannoli tube, sealing the edge with a bit of egg white.

Heat the oil in a deep-fat fryer or deep saucepan to 180°C (a small piece of bread dropped in will fizzle and turn brown straight away when dropped into the oil).

Fry the shells on the tubes, a few at a time, for 2–3 minutes or until golden and slightly puffy. Use tongs to turn them as you go. Carefully remove from the hot oil using the tongs and place on a wire rack set over kitchen paper. Cool just long enough so that you can handle the tube, then carefully twist it to remove the shell – using a tea towel may help you get a better grip. Wipe off the tubes and use them for shaping more shells.

Once cool, the shells can be kept in an airtight container for up to 2 months. Fill them no more than 1 hour before serving as they can get soggy.

To make the filling, stir together the ricotta cheese, icing sugar and vanilla, and fold in the candied fruits. Use a piping bag to pipe the filling into the shells, filling halfway from one end and then doing the same from the other end. Dip each end in the chopped pistachios, dust with icing sugar and serve.

Warm Wild Strawberry Crostata

Crostata are ubiquitous all over Italy in various shapes and forms and can be found with a variety of fillings. The Sicilians love to use the abundant citrus fruits found on the island to make marmalades and compotes to fill their *crostata*. My version was inspired by a bakery in Marsala which used the most incredibly fragrant wild strawberries, which were lightly cooked, with walnuts adding an appealing earthiness. Served warm this is divine, especially with cream or *gelato* – I like it with the Ricotta and Cream Ice Cream on page 271.

Serves 8–10

For the pastry
100g walnuts
250g '00' pasta flour
zest of 1 orange
120g golden caster sugar
1 tablespoon baking powder
a pinch of fine sea salt
120g unsalted butter, melted
3 free-range egg yolks

For the filling
500g wild strawberries (or hulled
    English strawberries, cut in half
    if large)
2 tablespoons caster sugar
150ml double cream
100g walnut halves

To make the pastry first blitz the walnuts in a food processor to a fine crumb. Transfer to a bowl and mix in the flour, zest, sugar, baking powder and salt. Make a well in the centre and mix in the butter and egg yolks to form a firm dough. Wrap the dough in clingfilm and chill for at least 1 hour before using.

Now make the pastry case. You'll need a 20cm loose-bottomed tart tin. As the dough is traditionally very crumbly it isn't rolled out. Instead, tear pieces off and press into the tin until it is fully lined – this will use about two-thirds of the dough. The pastry case will look rustic but that is the result you want. Chill in the freezer for 30 minutes to firm up.

Preheat the oven to 200°C/180°C fan/Gas Mark 6. While the pastry case is chilling, heat a large sauté pan over a medium heat. When hot throw in the strawberries and toss quickly to heat and start to release the juices. The berries may scorch a little, which is fine. Now sprinkle over the sugar and pour around the cream. Move the strawberries around in the pan, letting them brown in the sugar-cream mix, but be careful not to burn it. Reduce down to a thick jammy consistency with whole fruit pieces, then add the walnuts and remove from the heat.

Remove the tart case from the freezer. Line with baking parchment and weigh down with baking beans or rice. Blind bake for 12 minutes to seal. Remove from the oven and turn the oven down to 190°C/170°C fan/Gas Mark 5.

Remove the paper and beans from the pastry case. Spoon the strawberry mix into the tart case to fill. Pull pieces off the rest of the dough and crumble on to the filling, rustic style, leaving gaps here and there. Return the tart to the oven and bake for 30 minutes. Turn the oven down to 170°C/150°C fan/Gas Mark 3/4 and bake for a further 10 minutes. The top will have turned a deep golden brown and the fruit filling will be sticky and bubbling away inside. Serve the crostata just warm.

Flourless Orange Cake
with Marsala-orange caramel

The origin of this lovely cake lies with the Sephardi Jews of Spain. The recipe and technique stemmed from an abundance of nuts and a lack of wheat. Naturally gluten free with a delicious, crumbly texture.

I once ate an orange cake in a pastry shop in the mountain top town of Erice on Sicily's north-west corner; it had the exotic scent of cardamom. I've brought that scent into my recipe. A love letter to Tunisia just over the water. My version uses the slightly bitter Seville orange.

Serves 8–10

For the cake
2 medium unwaxed oranges
   (preferably Seville, if available)
6 free-range eggs, separated
225g caster sugar
1 tablespoon honey
300g ground almonds
¼ teaspoon fine sea salt
a handful of flaked almonds, toasted

For the caramel syrup
4 Seville oranges (or 4 ordinary
   oranges and 1½ lemons)
150ml sweet Marsala
2 cardamom pods, crushed
about 2 tablespoons demerara sugar
a pinch of fine sea salt
2 tablespoons diced candied
   orange peel

Put the oranges for the cake in a small pan and cover with water (the fruit will bob to the top). Cover and bring to the boil, then turn down the heat and simmer, turning once, for 1½–2 hours or until soft. Alternatively, you can microwave the oranges. Drain and cool slightly, then cut open to check for pips, removing any you find (Sevilles have a fair few). Blitz the oranges in a blender to a purée.

Preheat the oven to 200°C/180°C fan/Gas Mark 6. Grease and line a 23cm springform cake tin.

Beat the egg yolks with the sugar and honey until thick and pale, then fold in the ground almonds, followed by the orange purée until well combined. Whisk the egg whites with the salt until stiff peaks will form. Gradually fold into the cake mixture, being careful to knock out as little air as possible. Spoon into the tin and bake for 45–50 minutes or until it is firm on top.

Meanwhile, squeeze the fruit for the syrup into a saucepan and add the Marsala, cardamom, 1 tablespoon of the sugar and the salt. Bring to a simmer, stirring to dissolve the sugar, and cook for 5 minutes. Taste and add more sugar if you like. Stir in the candied peel, then allow to cool.

When the cake comes out of the oven, leave it in the tin and poke a few holes in the top with a skewer. Pour over the syrup a little at a time, and allow it to sink in. Scatter the flaked almonds over the surface. Leave to cool completely before transferring to a plate. Serve with mascarpone or a scoop of my Almond Milk Ice Cream on page 270.

Sweet Ricotta Torta
with dark chocolate and orange zest

I like to make this ricotta cake with *pasta frolla*, a soft, crumbly, sweet short pastry scented with orange zest. It's great for all manner of Italian pastry-based desserts such as *torte* and *crostate*. The bitter chocolate acts as a lovely contrast to the sweet tart filling.

Serves 8–10

For the pasta frolla
100g unsalted butter, chopped
zest of 1 orange
55g caster sugar
1 free-range egg
225g plain flour
½ teaspoon baking powder
a pinch of fine sea salt
2 teaspoons iced water

For the filling
450g fresh ricotta cheese
100g cream cheese, at room
 temperature
1 teaspoon vanilla extract
110g caster sugar
2 free-range eggs
100g 70% dark chocolate
icing sugar for dusting

To make the pastry, beat the butter, half the orange zest and the sugar with an electric mixer until smooth and combined. Beat in the egg. Fold in the flour, baking powder, salt and iced water to make a dough. Wrap in clingfilm and chill for 2 hours.

Preheat the oven to 220°C/200°C fan/Gas Mark 7.

Roll out the pastry between 2 sheets of baking parchment to about 3mm thickness. Use to line the bottom and side of a 22cm loose-bottomed, fluted tart tin, trimming off any excess. Chill in the freezer for 10 minutes.

Line the pastry case with baking parchment and weigh down with baking beans (or rice). Set the tin on a baking tray and blind bake the pastry case for 20 minutes or until the edges are light golden. Remove the beans and paper, then bake for a further 10 minutes or until the base is golden. Remove from the oven and cool slightly. Reduce the oven temperature to 170°C/150°C fan/Gas Mark 3/4.

To make the filling, beat the ricotta with the cream cheese using an electric mixer until smooth. Beat in the vanilla extract, remaining orange zest, the caster sugar and eggs. Pour into the tart case. Bake for 30 minutes or until the pastry is golden and the filling is set but with a gentle wobble in the centre.

Cool to room temperature, then chill for 2 hours. Grate over the chocolate with a microplane or very fine grater and dust with icing sugar before serving.

Strawberry, Almond and Rosewater Cake
with mascarpone

A creation reminiscent of the elaborate cakes found in Palermo's grand cafés. This almond-based version is surprisingly light. The rose element is subtle but permeates the cake adding an exotic Moorish perfume, and the rosewater works in harmony with the strawberries. I make this cake for dinner parties throughout the summer – it looks wildly decadent and is easy to make.

Serves 8–10

250g unsalted butter, softened
250g icing sugar
250g free-range eggs (4 large eggs)
200g plain flour, sifted
75g ground almonds
¼ teaspoon baking powder
150g fresh strawberries, hulled and
    cut in half
2 teaspoons rosewater

For the compote
150g strawberries, hulled and halved
40g caster sugar
½ teaspoon rosewater

To serve
candied rose petals (optional)
250g mascarpone whisked with
    45g caster sugar

Preheat the oven to 200°C/180°C fan/Gas Mark 6. Butter and line a 22cm springform cake tin.

In a stand mixer, whisk together the butter and icing sugar, slowly at first and then up to full speed until light and fluffy. Now, with the mixer on medium speed, add the eggs, one at a time, and then the sifted flour followed by the ground almonds and baking powder. Finally, fold in the strawberries and rosewater.

Spoon the mixture into the cake tin. Bake for about 50 minutes or until the cake is golden brown and a skewer inserted into the centre comes out clean. Remove from the oven and cool before removing from the tin.

While the cake is cooling, make the compote: place the strawberries and sugar in a saucepan and cook gently until the fruit breaks down and the juices thicken and turn jammy. Remove from the heat and cool, then stir in the rosewater. Reserve.

To serve, portion the cake, spoon over the compote and top with candied rose petals, if using. Spoon a dollop of sweetened mascarpone on the side.

Bitter Chocolate Torta
with walnuts and dates (tenerina-style)

Tenerina means 'delicately soft' and the chocolate filling for this *torta* is certainly *tenerina*. This style of cake originated in Ferrara in northern Italy and spread throughout Italy with regional spins. My version is based on one I tried in Sicily. Whilst the filling is *tenerina*, I've lightly baked it into a pastry crust to give a nice crunch. The cake is finished with some sticky dates and toasted, salted walnuts. This is the most delicious *torta* made exceptional by the addition of a scoop of ice cream or a dollop of mascarpone.

Serves 8–10

1 quantity of pasta frolla (see Sweet Ricotta Torta, page 239), at room temperature
225g bitter chocolate
225g unsalted butter
zest of 1 small orange

6 free-range eggs
250g caster sugar
150ml Marsala superiore
50g Medjool dates, stones removed and chopped
70g walnut halves, chopped

Preheat the oven to 220°C/200°C fan/Gas Mark 7. Roll out the pastry between 2 sheets of baking parchment to about 3mm thickness. Use to line the bottom and side of a non-stick 23cm springform cake tin, trimming off any excess. Chill the pastry case in the freezer for 10 minutes.

Line the pastry case with baking parchment and weigh down with baking beans (or rice), then place on a baking tray. Blind bake for 20 minutes or until the edges are light golden. Remove the beans and paper, and bake for a further 10 minutes or until the case is golden.

Remove from the oven and set aside to cool slightly. Reduce the oven temperature to 160°C/140°C fan/Gas Mark 3.

Melt the chocolate and butter in a bain marie or heatproof bowl set over a saucepan of hot water, then stir in the orange zest.

Whisk the eggs with an electric mixer until light and airy and doubled in volume. Whisk in 200g of the caster sugar. Fold the chocolate-butter mix into the eggs, in 3 stages, until fully incorporated. Transfer the chocolate mix to the pastry case and smooth the top as necessary.

Place in the oven and bake for 25 minutes or until the filling has started to set around the edges but still has a wobble in the middle. Remove from the oven and allow to cool before removing from the tin.

While the torta is baking, pour the Marsala into a saucepan and stir in the remaining 50g of sugar. Set over a high heat and boil until reduced to a syrup. Stir in the dates and walnuts, and set aside to cool.

Spoon the syrup over the top of the cooled torta. Slice the torta into portions and serve with the Ricotta and Cream Ice Cream on page 271.

Sweet Rice Fritters
with orange blossom honey

The Sicilian name of these fritters is *crespelle di riso alla benedettina*, because they were prepared in the Benedictine Monastery of Catania, a jewel from the late Baroque period, and traditionally eaten on Saint Joseph's Day. Nowadays though these fritters are eaten throughout the winter period and on Christmas day. As with many of Sicily's fried sweet delights, they are Arabic in origin. I confess I am addicted to them!

My version somewhat goes against the traditional grain as I've enriched the rice with mascarpone and butter and added yeast to make the fritters delicately light and fluffy.

Serves 4

300ml water
400ml full-fat milk
60g caster sugar
300g arborio rice
200ml mascarpone
75g unsalted butter
2 tablespoons milk

10g fresh yeast or a 7g sachet
  dried yeast
100g plain flour
zest of 1 orange
a pinch of ground cinnamon
1.5 litres sunflower oil for frying
200ml orange blossom honey

Combine the water, milk and sugar in a heavy-based pan and bring to the boil. Add the rice and cook over a medium heat, stirring with a wooden spoon, for about 20–30 minutes or until the rice is tender but still a bit firm. Pour the rice into a bowl and stir in the mascarpone and butter. Leave to cool completely.

Heat the milk until lukewarm and then add in the yeast and stir to dissolve. Add to the rice along with the flour, orange zest and cinnamon. Cover with clingfilm and set aside to rise for 1 hour or until doubled in size.

Tip the rice mixture on to a work surface. Use a wet knife to form it into a 1cm thick rectangle. Cut out batons, about 1cm thick and transfer to the fridge to chill for 10 minutes before frying.

Heat the oil in a deep-fat fryer or deep saucepan to 180°C (a small piece of the rice mix will fizzle when dropped into the oil).

Fry the rice fritters in batches, letting the rice batons fall directly into the hot oil as they are cut. Fry until golden, then drain on kitchen paper.

Heat the honey in a small saucepan. Place the rice fritters on serving plates and drizzle over the warm honey. Serve.

Iris

chocolate and ricotta-filled doughnuts

Fried sweet doughnuts are hugely popular all over Italy but none come close to the completely over-the-top Iris doughnuts of Sicily. Being Sicilian doughnuts, they are extra large and over stuffed with what can only be described as a sort of chocolate pudding.

These are a sure fire, sugar-laden short-term hangover cure, especially when followed with a double shot of Sicilian espresso at breakfast.

Serves 4

500g strong white flour
50g unsalted butter, softened
20g fresh yeast, dissolved in
    100ml warm water
50g caster sugar
a pinch of fine sea salt
1 free-range egg
250ml full-fat milk
icing sugar for dusting

For the filling
400g ricotta cheese
150g caster sugar
100g dark chocolate, grated

For frying
2 free-range eggs, beaten
300g very fine dried breadcrumbs
2 litres groundnut oil

First make the dough. Sift the flour into a bowl. Stir in the softened butter and then the yeast-water mix, caster sugar and salt. When fully combined, add the egg and milk. Continue to mix thoroughly until you achieve a soft but pliable and smooth dough. Cover the bowl with clingfilm and leave the dough to rise for 1½ hours or until doubled in size.

Meanwhile, make the filling. Mix together the ricotta and caster sugar, then stir in the grated chocolate. Reserve.

When the dough is ready, divide it into portions weighing about 100g. Roll out each portion on a floured surface to a circle about 1cm thick. Spoon some of the filling into the centre of each circle, then gather up the edges to form a small purse shape and press the gathered edges together to seal. Transfer the doughnuts, gathered edge facing downwards, to a tray lined with baking parchment. Leave to rise for 30 minutes.

Now dip the doughnuts in beaten egg and then coat all over with breadcrumbs, ensuring they are fully covered.

Heat the oil in a deep-fat fryer or deep saucepan to 170°C (a good pinch of breadcrumbs dropped in will fizzle and brown immediately). Cook the doughnuts, in 2 or 3 batches, in the hot oil until they are golden brown and crisp all over and warm in the middle. Drain well on kitchen paper, dust with icing sugar and serve immediately.

Sweet Pumpkin Sfinci
with grape must

There are many versions of this hole-less doughnut to be found across Sicily. Traditionally fried in pork fat, versions include the honey *sfinci*, which are dipped straight from the fat into a honey syrup, a potato-based version and various stuffings that includes an egg custard, a sweet cinnamon-spiced ricotta, lemon curd and chocolate. All are utterly delicious. My version is based on a recipe from the Aeolian islands which uses pumpkin as the base. Try to get a heavy fleshed pumpkin. I add juicy raisins and sultanas for pops of texture and fry in olive oil instead of lard. Defiantly serve with some whipped cream or mascarpone.

Serves 6

700g dense-fleshed pumpkin
  (or a butternut squash will do)
sea salt
5 tablespoons mixed raisins and
  sultanas, soaked in warm water
  to plump and drained
180g '00' pasta flour plus extra
  if needed
1 teaspoon dried yeast

a large sprig of rosemary, leaves picked
  and finely chopped
1.5 litres light extra virgin olive oil
  for frying
30g caster sugar
30g icing sugar
1 teaspoon ground cinnamon
about 100ml saba (grape must)

Cut the pumpkin into quarters (or the butternut squash in half) and peel. Scrape out the seeds and fibres, then cut the flesh into large chunks.

Put the chunks into a medium, heavy saucepan and sprinkle with salt. Cover and steam over a low heat without adding any water – there will be enough moisture in the pumpkin. Check every few minutes to be sure that the pumpkin isn't sticking to the bottom of the pan.

When the pumpkin is tender transfer to a blender and blitz to a smooth-ish purée. Turn out into a bowl.

Add the raisins to the pumpkin purée along with the flour, yeast and chopped rosemary, stirring with a wooden spoon until well combined. The batter should be stiff enough to hold the spoon upright. If necessary, add a little more flour. Cover the bowl with a tea towel and leave to rise in a warm place for an hour.

Heat the olive oil in a deep-fat fryer or deep saucepan to 170°C (a little dough dropped in will fizzle and crisp straightaway).

Fry the fritters in 2 or 3 batches: drop the batter a teaspoonful at a time into the hot oil. When the fritters are golden brown and puffed up, remove with a slotted spoon and drain on kitchen paper.

Combine the sugars with the cinnamon and sprinkle over a plate. Roll the hot fritters in the sugar mixture. Then either roll the fritters in the grape must or serve the grape must separately for dipping.

Sicilian Lemon Cream

with stewed mulberries or blackberries

Unlike similar puddings that use flours for thickening, this very simple posset-style pudding really showcases the zingy, fragrant flavour of the lemons. The mix of cream and mascarpone is not only rich and indulgent, but fresh too. Unwaxed lemons will give the best flavour. I like to make this in the early winter months when Sicilian and Amalfi lemons are bursting into season.

Mulberries aren't as common in the UK as they are in Europe but if you can find them, perhaps in a Middle Eastern supermarket or a specialist fruiterer, they are utterly delicious. They resemble an elongated blackberry with denser flesh and a singular sweet-sour aromatic flavour. Blackberries will make a very good alternative.

Serves 4

For the lemon cream
2 large unwaxed lemons with
    unsprayed leaves
150g caster sugar
150ml double cream
300g mascarpone

For the berries
250g mulberries or blackberries
150ml good red wine
60g golden caster sugar
1 tablespoon honey

Zest the lemons and squeeze the juice; you need 80ml juice. Put the lemon zest and 80ml juice in a saucepan with the sugar. Heat over a medium-low heat, stirring until the sugar has dissolved completely. Remove from the heat and keep warm.

In a separate pan, heat the cream and mascarpone over a medium-low heat, bringing just to a simmer – do not let it boil (otherwise it may separate). Remove from the heat, add the lemon mixture and whisk. Cool slightly, then strain through a fine sieve into bowls. Cool completely, then leave in the fridge for at least 8 hours or until firm and chilled.

While the lemon cream is chilling, prepare the stewed berries. Place the fruit in a saucepan, just cover with water and add the wine, sugar and honey. Bring to the boil, then simmer for 10 minutes or until the fruits are very tender but still holding their shape. Use a slotted spoon to remove the fruits from the liquid to cool. Boil the remaining liquid until syrupy. Let this cool, then pour over the berries. Chill.

To serve, spoon some of the berries on to each cream. Delicious with biscotti.

Watermelon Jelly

with jasmine, chocolate and pistachios

This is a stunning yet simple Moorish-inspired recipe with its roots dating back to the Middle Ages. A Moorish version of this vivid pink 'jelly' would have been the height of sophistication, prepared by skilled Arab chefs for the aristocracy and the wealthy. I find the garishness of it utterly charming in the Sicilian way.

I played around with this and tried using gelatine so that it firmed up to resemble something closer to what we know as jelly, but I eventually came to the conclusion that using corn starch instead created a more interesting texture, more like a pudding than a jelly.

Success relies heavily on the quality of the watermelon. Enjoy this pudding in the summer months when watermelons are at their most juicy and sweet.

Serves about 10

1 small or ½ large watermelon (2.5–3kg)
a handful of unsprayed jasmine flowers, plus some for decoration
150–200g caster sugar (depending on the sweetness of the watermelon)

70g cornflour
20g bitter chocolate chips
a handful of bright green pistachios (such as Bronte or Iranian), chopped

Peel the watermelon, then coarsely chop the pulp or pulse in a food processor. Pass through a fine-mesh sieve to extract the juice; discard seeds and thicker pulp. You need 1 litre of juice.

Add the jasmine flowers to the watermelon juice and set aside to steep for 3 hours.

Strain the juice and discard the flowers. Pour the juice into a saucepan, add the sugar and whisk in the cornflour. Cook over a low heat, whisking constantly, until the mixture comes to the boil. Reduce the heat and stir until thickened enough to coat the whisk. Pour the mix into a bowl, glasses or moulds and chill until cold and set.

If you are unmoulding the jellies, dip the moulds briefly in hot water, then turn out the jellies. Before serving, garnish with chocolate chips, chopped pistachios and jasmine flowers.

Limoncello Semifreddo
with cherries

Semifreddos are very popular in the south of Italy; they are much lighter and more delicate than ice creams, and they don't need churning. This one is scooped but you could put it into a mould to set and then cut off slices. The limoncello is important here – I recommend a good, fresh-flavoured cloudy variety such as Il Convento. The addition of lightly marinated cherries acts as a deliciously juicy foil to the limoncello.

Serves 4

4 large free-range eggs
75g caster sugar
500ml double cream
150ml limoncello, plus extra
   4 tablespoons

500g ripe cherries, cut in half and
   stones removed
zest of 1 large unwaxed lemon
2½ tablespoons lemon juice
4 tablespoons icing sugar

Separate the eggs into 2 large mixing bowls. Add the caster sugar to the egg yolks and beat for a few minutes with an electric mixer until pale and thick. Using clean beaters, whisk the egg whites in the other bowl to stiff but not dry peaks.

In another bowl, whip the cream to soft peaks. Fold the cream into the egg yolks, then fold in 150ml limoncello. Carefully fold in the egg whites.

Spoon the mixture into a shallow 2.5 litre serving dish that is about 5cm deep. Cover with clingfilm and freeze for at least 7–8 hours.

About 30 minutes before serving, put the cherries into a bowl. Add the lemon zest and juice, the icing sugar and the extra 4 tablespoons limoncello. Gently stir together, then cover and chill for 20 minutes.

To serve, scoop large spoonfuls of the semifreddo on to dessert plates and spoon some of the cherries alongside. Serve immediately as semifreddo melts faster than normal ice cream.

granita
&
ice creams

It's no exaggeration to say that the desserts of Sicily are famed the world over and perhaps none more so than those that refresh and revive the body and soul amidst the island's scorching heat– the *granita* and the *gelato*.

One of my greatest pleasures when in Sicily is to sit outside a shaded bar or café and sample the wonderful *gelato* and *granita* on offer whilst watching the world busy itself in the blistering summer heat.

The *granita* is perhaps Sicily's greatest culinary gift to the world – the incredibly refreshing shavings of ice sublimely flavoured with fruit juices, coffee, almonds, or indeed anything that comes to hand and that seems right and delicious.

Atop the frozen peaks of Mount Etna and the surrounding mountains are to be found man-made, insulated centuries-old stone snow huts. Snow and ice was gathered and stored in these stone huts through the winter months ready for distribution in ice blocks to bars, cafés and restaurants across Sicily, where they would then be shaved into refreshing flavoured precursor to *granita*.

It was an extraordinary means of production from a gift of nature that produced equally extraordinary culinary results.

The Arab occupation of Sicily saw sugar, herbs and spices added to the snow, and then during the sixteenth century, the Sicilians began to experiment with ways to produce what we now recognise as *granita*, essentially using a wooden barrel with a metal bucket inside. Snow and salt would be packed into the space between the two, freezing the mixture in the bucket.

But as the world moved on, so too did the means of production of *granite*, and eventually electrically powered ice makers replaced the traditional techniques.

Head to Sicily at any time of year and you'll find the bars and cafés serving all manner of delicious, exciting flavoured *granite*, eaten for breakfast, lunch and dinner in a glass or sandwiched between brioche. Such is the ritual that come rain or shine, chill or heat, the *granita* is always in demand.

And sitting proudly alongside *granita* as Sicily's great gift to the world of iced confections is the *gelato*, Sicily's wonderful version of ice cream. Introduced to the island by the Arabs, it took Sicily, and later the rest of the world, by storm. Addictive, versatile and utterly delicious, the Sicilians are still consuming it in large quantities to this day.

The ice creams in this chapter can be made without a machine; however, this will never be as smooth as a machine-churned *gelato*. Put the mixture into a freezerproof container and freeze for 45 minutes, then whisk well and return to the freezer. Repeat the whisking several times, every 45 minutes or so, until you have an ice cream consistency.

Coffee Granita
with whipped cream

The first time I tried coffee *granita* with whipped cream was on one of my earliest visits to Sicily when staying in rather a grand hotel in Taormina. The spectacular breakfast buffet had a *granita* station with several different *granite* stored in antique silver cool flasks with various suitable accompaniments – chopped pistachio, whipped cream, candied orange zest. I was fascinated and made the most of it every morning. It wasn't until my last day that I saw a fellow guest stuffing the espresso *granita* and whipped cream into a sweet brioche bun like a big, overblown sandwich. I followed the man's example. Deliciously over the top, not for the faint hearted, definitely well worth trying and quintessentially Sicilian!

Serves 8

80g ground espresso coffee (or 1 litre freshly brewed espresso)
1 litre water
80g caster sugar
1 tablespoon lemon juice

To serve
300ml whipping cream
3 tablespoons icing sugar
brioche buns, home-made (see Sicilian Brioche, page 26) or shop-bought

Put the ground coffee in a pan with the water. Bring to the boil, stirring occasionally, then remove from the heat. Leave to brew for a few minutes, then pour through a coffee filter or a sieve lined with muslin into a bowl or jug. Stir the sugar into the hot coffee to dissolve. Add the lemon juice. Allow to cool, then taste for sweetness.

Chill in the fridge for 1 hour before transferring to a freezerproof container and freezing for 1 hour. Remove, whisk and return to the freezer. Continue freezing, whisking every 20–30 minutes, to form frozen crystals and prevent a solid frozen lump. Once the granita is ready, it can be kept in the freezer for 3 days – no longer or it will lose its flavour.

Whip the cream to soft peaks, whisking in the icing sugar at the end.

Serve the coffee granita in glasses topped with whipped cream or stuffed into brioche buns.

Buttermilk Granita

This is one of my favourite *granite*. Delicious and refreshing. Some would say that as it has a dairy element it's not really an authentic *granita*. Either way, the natural lactic tang of buttermilk suits the process perfectly.

Serves 8–10

950ml buttermilk
150g caster sugar
½ teaspoon fine sea salt

Whisk together the buttermilk, sugar and salt in a bowl until the sugar has dissolved. Pour this granita base into a shallow freezerproof container and freeze for about 30 minutes to start setting.

Stir the granita base with a fork, breaking up the ice crystals to keep it from forming a solid mass (it will begin freezing around the edges first; mix the broken ice bits into the centre). Return to the freezer.

Every 30 minutes, mix the granita base to break up the ice crystals until it is completely frozen – this will take about 3 hours. Cover and keep in the freezer until ready to serve (up to 3 days).

Use a fork to scrape the buttermilk granita into a soft, snowy mixture just before serving.

Sicilian Lemon Granita
with mint

This *granita* is all about the lemon. So be sure to get the large knobbly varieties that are packed with flavour, such as those from Amalfi or Sicily. This *granita* should knock you over with sheer citrus power. My recipe is inspired by Kitty Travers of La Grotta Ices – the best that I know. The soda water is a nice little touch and gives extra pep to this king of *granite*.

For the ultimate retro-presentation serve in a hollowed-out, frozen lemon shell and top with a dollop of mascarpone.

Serves 8–10

7 large Amalfi or other quality
   unwaxed lemons
190ml water

150ml soda water
190g golden caster sugar
a handful of mint

Zest 4 of the lemons. Squeeze the juice from all the lemons – you want about 500ml.

Put the water, soda water and sugar into a saucepan with the lemon zest and mint. Bring to the boil, stirring until the sugar dissolves, then simmer for a minute to infuse. Remove from the heat and cool.

Strain into a bowl to remove the mint and zest. Stir in the lemon juice and then pour into a shallow freezerproof container and freeze for 4–5 hours. Stir the granita every so often so that it doesn't freeze into a solid lump (you want the consistency to be a little granular). Once frozen, break up into small pieces with a fork, then return to the freezer. After another hour, break it up again, then serve.

Strawberry Granita

Fragrant summer strawberries work perfectly in a *granita*. Add a dollop of whipped cream or infuse the base with a few basil stalks for a nice flavour twist.

Serves 6–8

450g fresh ripe strawberries, hulled
175g caster sugar

570ml water
juice of 2 lemons

Put the strawberries into a blender and blitz to a smooth purée. Add the sugar and blend again very briefly. Add the water and lemon juice, and blend once more.

Pour the purée into a fine nylon sieve set over a bowl. Rub the purée through the sieve, then pour it into a freezerproof container. Cover and freeze for 2 hours. By this time the mixture should have started to freeze around the sides and bottom.

Take a large fork and mix the frozen mixture into the unfrozen. Cover, return to the freezer and freeze for 1 hour. After that repeat the vigorous mixing with a fork. Cover again and freeze for another hour.

At this stage the granita should be a completely frozen snow of ice crystals, and it is ready to serve. It can remain at this servable stage in the freezer for a further 3–4 hours, but after that the ice will become too solid. The granita will need to be transferred to the fridge to soften for 30–40 minutes or until it can be broken up with a fork again.

Watermelon Granita

As if watermelons weren't refreshing enough, turning them into a frosty *granita* takes their freshness to a new level. The vivid pink ice crystals are wonderfully appealing on a hot summer's day. Try adding a few drops of rosewater to the cooled mix and finish with a dollop of creamy mascarpone.

Serves 6–8

1 small, heavy watermelon
  (about 1.3kg)
50ml orange juice

250g caster sugar
25ml lemon juice

Peel the watermelon, cut into chunks and blitz in a blender to a purée. Pass the juice through a fine-mesh sieve. You need 800ml juice.

Heat the orange juice and sugar in a saucepan over a low heat, stirring to dissolve the sugar. Remove from the heat and cool, then stir in the watermelon and lemon juices.

Pour into a freezerproof container and freeze for an hour. Remove and whisk the frozen sides and bottom into the unfrozen mixture. Put back into the freezer and freeze for a further 20–30 minutes, then whisk again. Continue freezing and whisking like this to form frozen crystals. It's now ready to serve.

As the granita is so fresh, do not keep it for longer than 3 days, otherwise it will lose its flavour.

Almond Milk Ice Cream

This is a proper Sicilian-style egg-free *gelato*. You could, at a pinch, use shop bought almond milk for this ice cream but there's a freshness captured in my recipe that can't be replicated out of a carton I'm afraid, so it's worth the little extra effort.

The apricot kernels add a bittersweet edge to the milk – you can buy them from health food shops or online.

Makes about
1 litre

200g caster sugar
800ml water
4 apricot kernels or 5g ground apricot
  kernels (optional)

150g blanched almonds
200ml double cream
a splash of orange blossom water

Make a sugar syrup by dissolving the sugar in the water, then boiling for 10 minutes or until syrupy and thick.

Pour the warm syrup into a blender, add the apricot kernels, if using, and the almonds, and blitz for 10 minutes or so, until nice and smooth.

Strain through a muslin-lined sieve into a bowl to separate the almond milk from the solids (discard the solids). Whisk the almond milk with the cream and orange blossom water. Cool completely before transferring to an ice-cream machine and churning to a whipped-cream consistency. Transfer to the freezer to set for at least 2 hours before serving.

Ricotta and Cream Ice Cream

Ricotta ice cream is a very Sicilian thing, often topped with candied fruits, nuts and preserved wet cherries in the *cassata* style. Leaving the custard in the fridge overnight helps the delicate ricotta flavours develop.

Makes about 800ml

400ml full-fat milk
220g caster sugar
3 free-range egg yolks

250g fresh ricotta
150ml double cream
1 tablespoon grappa (optional)

Place the milk and half the sugar in a saucepan and bring to just below the boil. Remove from the heat and leave for 10 minutes.

Set up a pan of boiling water for a bain marie. Put the egg yolks and remaining sugar in a heatproof bowl and set over the bain marie. Whisk together until pale, fluffy and thickened.

Bring the milk back to the boil and gradually whisk into the egg mix – do this slowly to avoid curdling.

Pour the whole mix back into the saucepan and heat gently until thickened like a custard, stirring constantly to prevent splitting. Remove from the heat and cool for a few minutes, then whisk in the ricotta bit by bit. Transfer to a container and chill overnight in the fridge.

Whisk in the cream and grappa, if using, then churn in an ice-cream machine until it takes on a whipped-cream consistency. Transfer to a freezerproof container and freeze for at least 2 hours before using.

Triple Chocolate Ice Cream

I've always had a thing for chocolate ice cream and many years ago set myself a little quest to find the best. This version is inspired by one from the glorious Gelato 2 in Palermo – the best place to buy *gelato* in Sicily and probably in Italy. The three chocolate elements make it a knock out in flavour and texture. This is now my personal favourite ... until the next one!

Makes 750ml

100g quality dark chocolate
    (minimum 70%), chopped
3 free-range egg yolks
200g caster sugar
500ml full-fat milk

50ml double cream
2 tablespoons cocoa powder
a large pinch of fine sea salt
30g cocoa nibs

Melt the chocolate in a bain marie or a heatproof bowl set over a pan of hot water, then allow to cool for 5 minutes. Reserve.

Whisk the egg yolks with the sugar using an electric mixer until smooth. Reserve.

Pour the milk, cream and cocoa powder into a saucepan and place over a medium heat. When almost boiling, remove from the heat and, beating constantly, add the melted chocolate. Slowly add this mixture to the egg yolk and sugar mixture, beating vigorously.

Pour back into the saucepan and cook over a very low heat, stirring with a wooden spoon (don't allow the mixture to boil) for 2–3 minutes or until the chocolate custard has thickened enough to coat the back of the spoon. Add the salt and mix well. Strain the custard through a fine sieve into a container. Cover and chill until completely cool.

Pour the chocolate custard into an ice-cream machine and churn. About 10 minutes before the gelato is ready stir in the cocoa nibs. Transfer the ice cream to a freezerproof container and freeze for at least 4 hours before serving.

Pumpkin Seed Ice Cream

I love this green ice cream. It has a sweet-bitter edge and is delicious served with some fresh, ripe blackberries or mulberries. And this is a brilliant way to use up delicious pumpkin seeds as an alternative to sprinkling them over a salad.

Makes about 800ml

1 vanilla pod
700ml full-fat milk
100g caster sugar
45g cornflour

200g pumpkin seeds
a pinch of fine sea salt
6 tablespoons extra virgin olive oil
3 tablespoons hot water

Split the vanilla pod and place it in a saucepan with the milk and 50g of the sugar. Stir through. In a small bowl, whisk a ladleful of the milk mix into the cornflour, ensuring there are no lumps.

Heat the milk mix in the pan over a medium heat and, when hot, whisk in the cornflour mix. Cook until thickened, stirring as you go. This should take about 5 minutes – do not let the mix boil otherwise it may split. Remove from the heat.

Toast the seeds in a dry sauté pan over a medium heat. Toss them occasionally as you go. Once they've released their oils and smell nutty, transfer to a blender and blitz with the remaining 50g sugar and the salt. Blend for 2 minutes, then add the oil and hot water. Continue to blend to produce a thick, smooth paste.

Whisk the seed paste into the thickened milk mix. Chill until completely cold before churning in an ice-cream machine. Transfer to a freezerproof container, cover and freeze for at least 2 hours before scooping for serving.

Fig Leaf Ice Cream

Fig leaves are heavy on the trees in Sicily from the spring through the summer months.

Sicilians use fig leaves for all sorts of food things – wrapping meats, for drying and burning over coals to flavour grilled fish and for infusing syrups and creams. This ice cream is fresh and figgy. I love it paired with fruits, either fresh and ripe or lightly roasted with honey.

Makes about 1 litre

600ml double cream
300ml full-fat milk
12 unsprayed fig leaves, torn

6 free-range egg yolks
125g caster sugar

Put the cream and milk in a saucepan with the torn fig leaves. Bring to a gentle simmer, then remove from the heat and leave to infuse for 1 hour.

Meanwhile, whisk the egg yolks with the sugar in a bowl until pale and smooth.

Bring the milk and cream back up to simmering point. Pour over the egg mixture, whisking all the time. Return the mixture to the saucepan, set it over a low heat and cook, stirring constantly with a wooden spoon, until the custard coats the back of the spoon.

Pass the custard through a fine sieve into a bowl. Leave to cool completely, then churn in an ice-cream machine. Transfer to a freezerproof container and store in the freezer for at least 2 hours before serving.

Fresh Mint Ice Cream

I am a fan of fresh mint in ice creams. Finely grate some bitter chocolate over the top and you will have a perfect summer iced dessert.

Makes about 700ml

300ml full-fat milk
250ml double cream
1 vanilla pod, split

100g caster sugar
3 free-range egg yolks
5 sprigs of mint

Put the milk, cream, vanilla and half the sugar in a saucepan and bring to just below the boil. Remove from the heat and set aside to infuse for 10 minutes.

Set up a pan of boiling water for a bain marie. Put the egg yolks and remaining sugar in a heatproof bowl, set over the bain marie and whisk until pale, fluffy and thickened.

Bring the milk back to the boil, then gradually whisk into the egg mix – add the hot milk slowly to avoid the mix curdling. Now remove the vanilla pod.

Pour the mix back into the saucepan and heat gently, stirring constantly to prevent splitting, until the custard has thickened. Remove from the heat and immediately add the mint sprigs. Stir through, then cool completely.

Remove the mint sprigs, then churn in an ice-cream machine to a whipped-cream consistency. Transfer to a freezerproof container and leave in the freezer for at least 2 hours before serving.

sauces
& basics

Salsa Verde

The classic multi-use green sauce. I love this with everything, especially grilled meat and fish.

*Makes about
200ml*

½ handful of flat-leaf parsley
   (with stalks)
½ handful of mint
½ handful of chives
2 teaspoons capers, drained
2 salted anchovies

1 tablespoon red wine vinegar
juice of ½ lemon
120ml extra virgin olive oil
sea salt and freshly ground
   black pepper

Put the herbs, capers and anchovies into a jug blender with the vinegar, seasoning and lemon juice. Start to blend, then, with the machine running, add the olive oil in a steady stream. You should end up with a thick, green, rustic sauce.

Pilacca
Sicilian-style Roasted Chilli Sauce

Pilacca is a wonderfully versatile southern Italian/Sicilian chilli sauce. Once made and steeped, it will keep for up to a month in a sealed jar. I love it stirred into ragùs or spooned over tomatoes on a bruschetta.

*Makes about 1
litre*

600ml extra virgin olive oil
12 fresh, long red chillies,
   ends removed
3 garlic cloves, finely chopped

1 tablespoon caster sugar
75ml red wine vinegar
sea salt and freshly ground
   black pepper

Heat half of the oil in a frying pan over a medium heat. When hot add the chillies and fry until they are blistered and soft. Remove from the oil and drain on a kitchen towel.

When cool, chop the chillies roughly and transfer to a bowl. Add the garlic, sugar and vinegar. Season well. Stir, then pour over the remaining oil. Cover the bowl and leave for at least 24 hours before using. For longer storage, transfer to a kilner-type jar and keep in the fridge for up to a month.

Gremolata

A multi-purpose salsa that's great with fish, meat or tossed through a simple pasta dish. Traditionally this is a dry mix, but I add oil and lemon juice to create something more akin to a lightly thickened dressing. You can play around with this recipe quite a bit, using orange instead of lemon, adding finely grated horseradish as an addition or changing the herbs to rosemary and thyme for a stronger, more robust flavour.

Makes about 175ml

2 tablespoons finely chopped flat-leaf parsley
1 tablespoon finely chopped marjoram or oregano leaves
1 garlic clove, finely chopped
1 shallot, finely chopped
zest and juice of ½ unwaxed lemon
50ml extra virgin olive oil
sea salt and freshly ground black pepper

Mix everything together and season well. Leave for an hour before use.

Salmoriglio

This dressing is all about the lemons. Find the best variety you can for flavour and aroma, such as Amalfi, Sicilian or an organic, knobbly variety. Delicious spooned over hot grilled fish, meat or vegetables and as a dressing for anchovies.

Makes 500ml

2 garlic cloves, crushed in a pestle and mortar with some sea salt
200ml extra virgin olive oil
200ml water
100ml fresh lemon juice (2–3 lemons)
a handful of herbs such as marjoram
sea salt and freshly ground black pepper

Whisk together the garlic, oil, water and lemon juice. Season with salt and pepper, then leave for an hour so the flavours can develop.

When ready to use stir in the fresh herbs.

Almond and Tomato Pesto

This sunny, Sicilian version of pesto is versatile and delicious. Toss through just-cooked pasta, over grilled or steamed vegetables or with barbecued fish. I also slather it on fresh focaccia for a superb pre-dinner snack.

Makes about 250ml

50g blanched almonds
200g roasted tomatoes from a jar, drained
a handful of basil
1 tablespoon red wine vinegar
½ teaspoon dried chilli flakes
50ml extra virgin olive oil
40g Parmesan cheese, grated
sea salt and freshly ground black pepper

Toast the almonds in a large, dry sauté pan over medium-high heat, stirring frequently, for 3–5 minutes or until golden and fragrant. Allow them to cool slightly.

Transfer the almonds to a food processor and blitz until finely ground. Add the tomatoes, basil, vinegar and chilli flakes. With the machine running, drizzle in the oil in a steady stream until fully incorporated. Stir in the Parmesan and season well.

The pesto will keep in a jar in the fridge for at least 2 weeks.

Alioli and Almond Alioli

My aliolis are more akin to a mayonnaise. Rich, yet still punchy in flavour, but not as harsh as the basic garlic and oil combination.

Alioli is delicious with pretty much all savoury foods. As a dip for crispy squid, spooned over baking hot vegetables so that the garlicky richness of the alioli melts all over them, or with grilled or roasted meats. The alioli is a canvas waiting for culinary colour – fresh herbs of your choice, orange juice, molasses, chopped anchovies … the list is endless.

Makes about 200ml

1 large free-range egg yolk
½ teaspoon Dijon mustard
½ garlic clove, very finely chopped
100ml vegetable oil
100ml extra virgin olive oil

lemon juice
white wine vinegar
sea salt and freshly ground
   black pepper

Put the egg yolk in a mixing bowl along with the mustard and garlic. Begin whisking while slowly adding the oils to emulsify with the yolk. As the oils are incorporated into the yolk and the mixture starts to thicken, you can speed up the process. When all the oil has been added, season with salt, pepper, lemon juice and vinegar to taste.

Almond alioli
Finely chop the picked leaves from a sprig of rosemary. Mix with 1 tablespoon very finely chopped blanched almonds and 20ml (4 teaspoons) extra virgin olive oil in a mortar and pound with the pestle to make a coarse green paste. Proceed with the alioli recipe above, replacing 50ml of the olive oil with the almond-rosemary paste, adding it after the 2 oils have been whisked in. Chill for an hour before serving to let the flavours infuse.

Tomato Sauce

My tomato sauce recipe has been with me for years. It's great for ragùs, pasta sauces, pizza toppings and pretty much everything else. Buy the ripest tomatoes available.

Makes 1.2 litres

2 red onions, finely diced
2 garlic cloves, finely chopped
1 fresh red chilli, deseeded and
    finely chopped
olive oil for cooking
25g tomato paste

1kg plum tomatoes, chopped
1kg canned chopped tomatoes
100ml white wine vinegar
sea salt and freshly ground
    black pepper

Sweat the onions, garlic and chilli in olive oil in a large saucepan until soft. Stir in the tomato paste and cook over a low heat for a further 2 minutes. Add the fresh and canned tomatoes, season well and add the vinegar. Cook on a simmer for about 1 hour 20 minutes or until thick and tasty.

Blitz in a food processor until fairly smooth.

Pine Nut and Saffron Sauce

A favourite of the Aeolian islands, this is often served with grilled dishes as a type of condiment. It's quite addictive and works really well with grilled artichokes and courgettes. Its heritage is Moorish and similar sauces are to be found all over Morocco and Tunisia.

Makes 250ml

175ml almond milk
1 garlic clove, peeled
1 fresh red chilli, cut in half
a good pinch of saffron threads
150g pine nuts, lightly toasted

50ml extra virgin olive oil
lemon juice
sea salt and freshly ground
    black pepper

Put the almond milk, garlic and chilli in a saucepan and bring to a simmer. Cook for 5 minutes. Add the saffron, then remove from the heat and leave to infuse for 20 minutes.

Strain the milk into another saucepan. Add the pine nuts, bring back to a simmer and cook for 5 minutes. Transfer to a blender and blitz until smooth. Add the olive oil and lemon juice to taste. Season and blitz again to incorporate.

Garlic Sauce

This garlic sauce has a wonderful depth and aroma. I use it as a base for pizzas. Also, if diluted with a little stock, it makes for a great simple pasta sauce. Alternatively use it as a dip for flatbreads and grilled meats.

Makes about 200ml

10 garlic heads/bulbs,
  tops trimmed slightly
10 sprigs of thyme
100ml extra virgin olive oil plus extra
  for cooking

juice of ½ lemon
a handful of blanched almonds, soaked
  in milk for 1 hour and drained
sea salt and freshly ground
  black pepper

Preheat the oven to 190°C/170°C fan/Gas Mark 5.

Place the garlic on an oven tray with a sprig of thyme on each bulb. Season and drizzle liberally with oil. Cover the tray with foil and roast the garlic for 1 hour or until the bulbs are very tender. Remove the foil and roast for a further 15 minutes or until caramelised.

Allow to cool, then squeeze the roasted cloves out of the garlic bulbs into a blender. Add the lemon juice, the 100ml of olive oil and the almonds. Blitz for 6–7 minutes or until you have a smooth, emulsified sauce. This will keep in the fridge for up to a month.

Pan Grattato

Pan grattato is essentially fried breadcrumbs, adored by Sicilians and added to a wide variety of dishes – pasta, salads, seafood, grilled meats – for crunch, flavour and to soak up excess tasty juices. So much more than the sum of its parts. I always have a bowl of this to hand.

Makes about 100g

50ml extra virgin olive oil
100g stale bread such as sourdough,
  crusts removed and blitzed or grated
  into crumbs (you can also used dried
  breadcrumbs such as panko)
sea salt

Simply heat the oil and fry the breadcrumbs until golden brown and crunchy. Season and drain. These can be kept in a covered container for up to a week.

Eggless Pasta Dough

This simple dough is traditional in southern parts of Italy where the climate calls for a dough that doesn't dry so quickly – most of the pasta dishes in the far south are made with dried eggless pasta.

*Makes about
550g to serve 4 as
a main course*

400g '00' pasta flour plus extra
   for dusting
100g semolina flour

½ teaspoon salt
about 300ml water to mix

Place the flours and salt in a bowl and slowly add the water, mixing as you go, until you have a dough that holds together. Dust it with flour, then knead in the bowl until the dough is smooth and firm. Wrap in clingfilm and chill for at least an hour before using.

Fresh Egg Pasta Dough

There are as many recipes for pasta dough as there are pasta shapes. I've used this recipe for years and it works very well. The addition of the semolina helps ease the rolling process and adds texture and integrity to the pasta. Use the very best eggs available – I like a very yellow yolk that will add colour to the pasta.

Makes about 600g to serve 4 as a main course

340g '00' pasta flour
160g semolina flour
a large pinch of salt

3 large free-range eggs plus 2 or 3 egg yolks, at room temperature

Mix together the 2 flours and the salt in a large bowl. Make a well in the middle. Lightly beat the eggs and 2 of the yolks together, then pour two-thirds of the mixture into the well in the flour.

Using your fingertips in a circular motion, gradually stir the flour into the eggs until you have a dough that you can bring together into a ball. If the mix doesn't come together then add the rest of the egg mix and then the third yolk if necessary. Knead for 10 minutes or until the dough is smooth and will spring back when pressed.

Divide the dough in half and wrap in clingfilm. Allow to rest in the fridge for an hour before rolling out and using as per your recipe.

index

about
the author

Classically trained with over 20 years' experience, Ben spent his formative career working with Michelin-starred chefs such as Jason Atherton and Stephen Terry at various ground-breaking London restaurants, learning classical techniques along with inspired culinary innovation. He went on to head up his own operations at the Italian restaurant Al Duca in St James, London, and the Crinan Hotel in the West Highlands. Under Ben's culinary leadership, the Crinan was awarded Best Gastro pub in Scotland by the *Independent* newspaper and Best Newcomer in the *Good Food Guide*.

Ben is now the Culinary Director of Norma on Charlotte Street and The Stafford London in St James, both in London's West End. At the Stafford London, Ben oversees the food offering throughout the hotel including the Game Bird restaurant, the American bar and private dining.

In September 2019 Ben opened Norma, a Sicilian–Moorish-influenced restaurant. The restaurant, which Ben opened in conjunction with The Stafford London, features a bespoke raw bar serving Sicilian-style *crudo* and a first-floor bar serving a selection of Marsala served by the glass.

Ben is a regular guest on *Saturday Kitchen*, *Sunday Brunch* and *MasterChef*, and writes for *Delicious*, the *Guardian*, *Telegraph*, *The Times*, *Noble Rot*, *Restaurant* magazine, *Chef* magazine and other publications.

Ben is an accomplished and award-winning food writer with three published cookbooks. *Moorish*, his last book, was published by Bloomsbury Absolute in April 2019, receiving critical acclaim including being named cook book of the year in the *Times Magazine*. This is his fourth book.

A regular cookery teacher at some of the UK's leading schools, including Leiths, Divertimenti, Cookhouse at Soho Farmhouse, Chewton Glen cooking school and Bertinet, teaching is one of Ben's passions.

Norma, the Sicilian-inspired restaurant I run in Fitzrovia. My key team members are lead by the brilliant chef Giovann Attard and Liz Reece.

Acknowledgements

Thanks to Nykeeta, my lovely wife, for all the patience, love and (selfless!) food tasting. Her opinion really means more than most others'. And the dogs, Piggy and new-ish recruit Peanut.

The entire, brilliant team involved with *Sicilia*. From Martine Carter, my friend and long-standing agent, to the best publishing team at Absolute: Jon Croft, Emily North, Meg Boas and Peter Moffat.

My mate and the best food photographer I know, Kris Kirkham, ably assisted by Eyder Rosso.

Giancarlo Vatteroni, my mate and long-standing colleague who has the unenviable job of deciphering my recipes and scribbled notes, and turning them into exactly what I want, as well as running around London in search of niche ingredients.

Leiths School of Food and Wine for providing brilliant cooks to help me make this a smooth, seamless operation: Shanika Basnayake, Lucy Rew and Jessica Mcintosh. There are great things to come for this team.

My team at Norma, led by the most talented Head Chef Giovann Attard, whose passion and drive is second to none, ably supported by Scott Whittaker. Liz Recce, ops manager, who holds everything together in the best way and Julienne Hennebelle for his wine and much more.

Stuart Procter, CEO of the Stafford Collection, once again for support and letting me get on with my food endeavours and guiding the company through the trickiest of times.

Jozef Rogulski, friend and Exec Chef at the Stafford, for always being there for me and with organisational skills I can only dream of.

My brilliant suppliers who kindly helped me on this project with the best produce, ingredients and equipment: Charlie Cook from Walter Rose butchers; Wellocks for the best vegetables and dried goods; Chapmans for the freshest fish; Carter Cherrill for the beautiful, seasonal flowers; Good Fellows for some of the gorgeous props we used during the shoot; and Ox Grills for their ingenious outdoor cooking grills (barbecue will never be the same again!). Thank you all.

Publisher
Jon Croft

Commissioning Editor
Meg Boas

Projects Editor
Emily North

Art Director
Peter Moffat

Designers
Peter Moffat
Marie O'Shepherd
Anika Schulze

Photographer
Kris Kirkham

Photographer's Assistant
Eyder Rosso

Food Stylists
Ben Tish with
Shanika Basnayake,
Jessica Mcintosh
and Lucy Rew

Home Economy
Adam O'Shepherd

Recipe Copyeditor
Norma MacMillan

Proofreader
Margaret Haynes

Indexer
Zoe Ross

BLOOMSBURY ABSOLUTE
Bloomsbury Publishing Plc
50 Bedford Square, London, WC1B 3DP, UK
29 Earlsfort Terrace, Dublin 2, Ireland

BLOOMSBURY, BLOOMSBURY ABSOLUTE, the Diana logo and the Absolute
Press logo are trademarks of Bloomsbury Publishing Plc.

First published in Great Britain 2021.

A catalogue record for this book is available from the British Library.

Library of Congress Cataloguing-in-Publication data has been applied for.

HB 9781472982759
ePub 9781472982742
ePDF 9781472982735

2 4 6 8 10 9 7 5 3 1

Printed and bound in China by C&C Offset Printing Co., Ltd.

Bloomsbury Publishing Plc makes every effort to ensure that the papers used in the
manufacture of our books are natural, recyclable products made from wood grown in
well-managed forests. Our manufacturing processes conform to the environmental
regulations of the country of origin.

To find out more about our authors and books visit
www.bloomsbury.com and sign up for our newsletters.